# THE ENTREPRENEUR'S BLUEPRINT: ACTIONABLE STRATEGIES FOR SUCCESS

TURNING AMBITION INTO ACTION: A GUIDE FOR DREAMERS AND DOERS

Rohan Kumar Bhoi

Made with ♥ on the Notion Press Platform
www.notionpress.com

My entrepreneurial journey began at the age of 17, a time when I was fuelled by ambition but lacked the knowledge and experience needed to navigate the complex world of business. Over the past four years, this journey has been anything but smooth. I have faced countless ups and downs, moments of self-doubt, and obstacles that tested my resilience. Yet, through every challenge, I learned, adapted, and grew. Today, as I write this book, I am still a student of entrepreneurship, eager to learn and evolve.

I decided to write The Entrepreneur's Blueprint: Actionable Strategies for Success to share the lessons I've gathered along the way. This book is not a guarantee of success - there's no magic formula for that - but it is a guide rooted in real-world experiences, designed to provide knowledge and perspective for those embarking on their own entrepreneurial journeys.

When I started, I wished for a mentor who could show me the way, someone who could explain not just the strategies but also the sacrifices and dedication required to achieve dreams. "Dreams don't work unless you do" became a mantra that kept me moving forward. Through this book, I hope to become that mentor for you, offering insights and actionable advice to help you navigate the unpredictable terrain of entrepreneurship.

Whether you are a student dreaming of starting your own business, a professional looking to take the leap into self-employment, or an entrepreneur seeking ways to refine your journey, this book is for you. It will guide you in building a solid foundation as a beginner and help seasoned entrepreneurs make their ventures more efficient and impactful.

This book is not about teaching everything there is to know. Frankly, I still have so much to learn myself. It is about sharing what I have discovered so far - what worked, what didn't, and what it truly takes to persevere in this dynamic, rewarding path. My hope is that these insights will inspire you to take action, embrace challenges, and make the compromises needed to bring your dreams to life.

So, let's embark on this journey together. As you turn the pages, I encourage you to reflect, adapt, and apply the lessons in ways that resonate with your unique aspirations. Success may not come overnight, but with dedication and the right mindset, the possibilities are endless.

**Welcome to The Entrepreneur's Blueprint. Let's build your future...**

# Content

# Foreword

As an entrepreneur, I've come to realize that there's no single blueprint for success. Every journey is unique, shaped by countless decisions, challenges, and lessons learned along the way. Yet, I often found myself wondering—what if there was a guide that could help others avoid common pitfalls, shorten the learning curve, and provide actionable strategies to navigate this demanding path?

That's exactly what ***The Entrepreneur's Blueprint* offers**.

This book is a culmination of my experiences - the victories, the setbacks, and the lessons that shaped me. Coming from humble beginnings in Rajegaon, Maharashtra, to building businesses that now thrive across industries, my journey hasn't been an easy one. But every challenge taught me something invaluable, and I believe those lessons deserve to be shared. From understanding the critical role of mindset to transforming ideas into actions that deliver impact, this book is my way of giving back to the entrepreneurial community.

What sets this book apart is its authenticity. These aren't theories or abstract concepts; they are insights drawn from my personal experiences. I don't claim to have all the answers, but I've been in the trenches. I've faced the doubts, embraced the risks, and celebrated the wins. ***The Entrepreneur's Blueprint*** reflects those truths.

Whether you're taking your first step into entrepreneurship or you're already walking the path, this book offers practical guidance and inspiration. I wrote it not just to share my story, but to remind you of what's possible. Entrepreneurship isn't just about building businesses; it's about pushing through challenges, staying true to your vision, and creating something meaningful.

If you're ready to elevate your journey, I'm excited to share this **blueprint** with you. Let's embark on this together. Your dreams are worth it.

**– Rohan Kumar Bhoi, Chairman**

SamaRoh Group of Business and Industries

# Preface

*"Success is not a destination; it's a journey fuelled by passion, perseverance, and the unwavering belief in your dreams."*

\- ***Rohan Kumar Bhoi***

**Author's Personal Journey**

Greetings! I'm Rohan Kumar Bhoi, the Founder and Chairman of Samaroh Group of Business and Industries. As I look back on my journey, I realize that it has been far from linear. My story is one of resilience, learning, and relentless pursuit—a journey of growth that continues with every new challenge I face. My life is a testament to the power of hard work, the courage to fail, and the undying belief that with enough persistence, anything is possible.

**The Journey**

I hail from Rajegaon, a small yet beautiful village nestled in the heart of Maharashtra, India. Raised in a humble fishing family, my upbringing was grounded in the values of dedication and hard work. These early experiences taught me that success is not handed to you—it's something you earn through consistent effort. From a young age, I nurtured a deep curiosity for technology, and it became the driving force of my life.

My academic journey began with a strong foundation in school. I completed my 10th grade with an impressive 90%, ranking first in my division. Despite the conventional route of moving to traditional 11th and 12th classes, I chose a different path that would change the course of my life: I opted for a diploma in computer engineering. This decision was pivotal, shaping the direction of my career and laying the groundwork for my entrepreneurial endeavors.

At Zeal College of Engineering, I excelled both academically and creatively, earning accolades for my innovative projects. My work in Project Mania competitions caught the attention of many, reinforcing my belief that creativity and technical expertise could go hand in hand. Graduating with a CGPA of 8.6, I confidently transitioned into the second year of computer engineering, self-funding my studies while balancing the demands of work and academics. It was a journey of grit and determination that shaped my future, and I was just getting started.

**Founding DevelopUs.tech**

Driven by a vision to merge creativity with technology, I founded **DevelopUs.tech**. From the outset, my goal was to transform ideas into digital masterpieces. As Founder, Chairman, and CEO, I blended my skills in programming with an innovative design philosophy to build web solutions that not only met but exceeded the expectations of our clients. Over the years, DevelopUs.tech has grown into a powerhouse in the field of web development, providing high-quality services and fostering a culture of innovation.

The journey hasn't been easy—there have been setbacks, failures, and lessons learned the hard way. But with every challenge, I've gained something invaluable. The strength to persevere, the resilience to bounce back from failure, and the knowledge to keep evolving. These experiences are the foundation of this book.

**Expanding Horizons**

In 2022, I expanded my vision even further by establishing the **Samaroh Group of Business and Industries**, which includes DevelopUs.tech, **RKL Worlds**, and **CompTT.tech**. These ventures have allowed me to solidify my leadership in both the tech industry and the manufacturing sector, providing new opportunities for growth, collaboration, and innovation. This expansion was a reflection of my ongoing commitment to creating value and leading with purpose.

**Vision and Values**

At the core of my entrepreneurial journey lies a passion for technology and a deep belief in the power of karma. At **DevelopUs.tech**, we don't just build websites—we help bring digital dreams to life. We provide clients with not just functional solutions, but experiences that inspire and drive success. Our commitment to creativity, quality, and innovation is what sets us apart in an ever-evolving industry.

My journey—from a small village to the top of the tech world—proves that extraordinary achievements are possible with unwavering dedication, the right mindset, and a passion for innovation. If a village boy like me can accomplish this, then anyone with the right drive can conquer their dreams. This book is a reflection of that belief—a guide for anyone willing to put in the work and follow their dreams, regardless of their background.

**Inspiration**

I wrote this book for those who, like me, are eager to take on the world of entrepreneurship but may not yet have the roadmap or the guidance to navigate it. I know the road is filled with challenges, and it's easy to get lost without proper direction. That's why I want to share what I've learned so far—so others can avoid some of the mistakes I made and learn from my experiences.

**Inspiration to Write**

Every entrepreneur faces ups and downs. I started my entrepreneurial journey without the proper knowledge, and it's been a continuous learning experience for the last four years. I began at the age of 17, diving headfirst into the business world with little more than passion and an idea. Since then, I've faced numerous challenges that tested my resolve, but I've never stopped learning. Through trial and error, I've gathered valuable knowledge about what it truly takes to succeed.

I know that I still have much to learn, and while I may not be in a position to teach seasoned entrepreneurs, I firmly believe that even those at the start of their journey can benefit from the insights I've gathered. This book is meant to guide students, professionals, and aspiring entrepreneurs. It's my way of paying forward the lessons I've learned and offering a guide to those who wish to embark on their own entrepreneurial journeys.

**Unique Perspective**

One of the biggest challenges we face today is the mindset that tends to steer young people toward traditional employment, rather than the path of entrepreneurship. Through this book, I want to shift that perspective. I want to show the youth of today that creating your own opportunities through entrepreneurship is not just a possibility—it's a path worth pursuing. There's power in thinking differently and taking risks.

My approach to entrepreneurship isn't about following the same old rules; it's about forging your own path. I believe that entrepreneurship requires more than just a business plan—it demands a mindset that is creative, resilient, and constantly evolving. My journey has taught me that success doesn't come from following the conventional route; it comes from the courage to break away and chart your own course.

**What Makes My Approach Distinct**

What makes my approach to entrepreneurship unique is that I blend technology with creativity and a deep commitment to solving real-world problems. I've always believed that business isn't just about profit—it's about making a meaningful impact. And this belief is woven into every project I undertake, whether it's in the tech space or the manufacturing industry. This book shares that philosophy with you, providing actionable insights, practical strategies, and an entrepreneurial mindset to help you succeed.

---

In this preface, I've shared my journey, my inspirations, and my unique perspective. Through this book, I want to inspire and guide you as you embark on your own entrepreneurial journey. There is no one-size-fits-all formula for success, but with the right mindset and the willingness to put in the work, you can achieve your dreams. It all starts with taking that first step. Let's begin this journey together.

# Acknowledgments

Writing this book has been a deeply personal journey, and there are many people and resources I am grateful to for supporting and inspiring me along the way.

First and foremost, I dedicate this book to my unwavering commitment to helping others. It is this desire to give back and share my experiences that has driven me to write. I believe in the power of knowledge and the importance of guiding others through the challenges I've faced on my own entrepreneurial path. My natural inclination to help and inspire others has shaped the vision for this book and has fuelled the countless hours spent crafting its content.

I would also like to express my gratitude to the many books that have guided me through this journey. Works *"The Subtle Art of Not Giving a F*ck", "The Power of Subconscious Mind", "Think and Grow Rich", "The Art of Letting Go", "The Richest Man In Babylon", "How to win Friends and Influence People", and my personal favourite, "Atomic Habits"*, have been invaluable sources of wisdom and inspiration. Each of these books offered unique insights that helped me refine my approach to entrepreneurship and personal development, and I'm forever grateful for the knowledge they provided.

Additionally, I want to acknowledge the powerful role that technology and artificial intelligence have played in bringing this book to life. My use of **ChatGPT** has enhanced the writing process, allowing me to refine my ideas and present them more effectively. While this book is based on my own experiences, AI has been an important tool in helping me express my thoughts more clearly and concisely.

While I did not rely on any specific organizations or institutions for the creation of this book, I must acknowledge the countless mentors, colleagues, and individuals I've met over the years. Their advice, encouragement, and support have been indispensable in shaping who I am today.

Finally, I would like to dedicate this book to two individuals whose influence has had a profound impact on my journey: **Sir Ratan Tata** and **Dr. APJ Abdul Kalam**. Their remarkable leadership, vision, and dedication to making a positive difference in the world have inspired me deeply. Sir Ratan Tata's integrity and commitment to innovation and Dr. Kalam's passion for inspiring the youth of India have shaped my entrepreneurial philosophy. This book is dedicated to their legacies, which continue to inspire me and countless others to pursue greatness with humility and purpose.

Thank you to everyone who has been part of my journey. Whether directly or indirectly, your presence has made this book possible.

# Prologue

Entrepreneurship is often portrayed as a glamorous journey—one of wealth, fame, and constant success. But in reality, it's far from that. The path of an entrepreneur is unpredictable, filled with highs and lows, triumphs and failures. It's a journey that requires more than just ambition; it demands resilience, adaptability, and a mindset that refuses to quit when faced with adversity.

I know this firsthand. My journey as an entrepreneur began at the age of 17, with little more than a vision and a deep desire to make something of myself. I had no roadmap, no guide, and no certainty about what the future would hold. All I had was my belief in the power of hard work and the desire to learn from every setback and challenge along the way.

Over the last four years, I've encountered my share of obstacles—mistakes, failures, moments of doubt. But with each setback, I've grown stronger. I've learned that entrepreneurship isn't about avoiding failure; it's about learning from it and using it as a stepping stone to something greater.

This book is not just for those who are starting their journey but also for those who have been on this path for years. It's a guide that draws from my own experiences—my successes, my failures, and everything in between. It's an invitation to explore the mindset, strategies, and lessons that have shaped my entrepreneurial journey, with the hope that you can apply them to your own path.

Throughout these pages, I share insights that have helped me navigate the challenges of entrepreneurship. I discuss the importance of mindset—how cultivating a resilient, growth-oriented mindset is crucial for overcoming the obstacles that will inevitably arise. I delve into the practical strategies that have helped me build and sustain businesses, offering a mix of personal stories and actionable advice.

But most importantly, I want you to understand that entrepreneurship is not a destination. It's a journey—one that requires passion, perseverance, and an unshakable belief in your ability to make a difference. It's about understanding that every challenge you face is an opportunity to grow, every failure is a lesson, and every success is a reminder of the power of your own determination.

If you've ever wondered whether you have what it takes to be an entrepreneur, this book will show you that you do. But success doesn't come overnight - it takes time, effort, and a willingness to keep going, even when the road ahead seems uncertain.

So, if you're ready to embark on your own entrepreneurial journey, or if you're looking to refine your existing path, this book is for you. Take the lessons from my experiences, apply them to your own journey, and remember: *dreams don't work unless you do*.

Welcome to ***The Entrepreneur's Blueprint*** - a guide to turning your dreams into reality.

# The Entrepreneur's Blueprint

## Actionable Strategies for Success

CHAPTER ONE

# The Entrepreneurial Mindset

The journey of entrepreneurship begins not with a groundbreaking idea or a revolutionary product, but with a shift in mindset - a perspective that propels you to see opportunities where others see obstacles, and to push forward when faced with uncertainty. This mindset is the bedrock of entrepreneurial success. It distinguishes dreamers from doers, wishful thinkers from achievers. It is a dynamic blend of vision, creativity, resilience, and adaptability - qualities that enable individuals to identify opportunities, overcome challenges, and create lasting value.

I've always believed that success isn't a destination; it's a journey. For me, this journey started in the small village of Rajegaon, Maharashtra, where I was born into a humble fishing family. Growing up in an economically weaker, middle-class environment, I learned early on the value of hard work, perseverance, and belief in my dreams. My story is a testament to the fact that the entrepreneurial mindset isn't something you're born with - it's something you cultivate through grit, determination, and a relentless pursuit of knowledge.

**The Core of the Entrepreneurial Mindset**

At the heart of the entrepreneurial mindset is creativity, resilience, and a relentless drive to innovate. It is not a trait you inherit, but one that you cultivate through intentional effort and practice.

**Visionary Thinking**

Entrepreneurs are visionaries who see possibilities where others see obstacles. They challenge the status quo, reimagine solutions, and uncover unmet needs. I remember when I started my first venture in web development, there were countless challenges. I was working in a highly competitive industry, but my ability to stay focused on my vision of providing high-quality web solutions helped me push forward. I saw an opportunity to fill a gap in the market and dedicated myself to mastering the technical and business aspects of web development. Despite the odds, I believed in my vision, and today, DevelopUs.tech stands as a symbol of what a clear, unwavering vision can achieve.

**How to Develop Visionary Thinking:**

Regularly practice imagining better versions of existing systems or products.

Spend time reflecting on how emerging trends could reshape industries.

**Resilience: Bouncing Back Stronger**

The entrepreneurial journey is rarely linear. It's filled with setbacks, failures, and unexpected hurdles. Resilience - the ability to bounce back stronger - is a cornerstone of the entrepreneurial mindset.

I've encountered numerous failures throughout my journey. There were moments when I felt like giving up. But every setback became an opportunity to refine my approach and learn from my mistakes. I remember when I first launched DevelopUs.tech, the early days were tough. We had to navigate through many obstacles - from understanding client needs to managing finances and balancing quality with delivery timelines. But I refused to let these setbacks define my journey. I redefined failure as a lesson and used each experience to fuel my next steps toward success.

**How to Build Resilience:**

Adopt a growth perspective: Treat failures as temporary and solvable.

Create a personal "bounce-back plan": Identify supportive practices (e.g., journaling, seeking advice) to help regain focus after setbacks.

**Grit: The Power of Perseverance**

Entrepreneurship isn't for the faint of heart. It requires grit - the passion and perseverance to chase long-term goals despite challenges. I learned this firsthand. In the early years of DevelopUs.tech, I worked relentlessly to prove my capabilities. There were countless moments when things weren't looking up, but my determination kept me going. As Jeff Bezos once said, "If you're not stubborn, you'll give up on experiments too soon." Perseverance became my compass, and slowly but surely, I began to see the fruits of my labor.

**Reflection:** Think of a challenge you overcame with sustained effort. What strategies helped you stay committed?

**Embracing Failure as a Learning Opportunity**

In many cultures, failure is stigmatized. But entrepreneurs understand that failure is not the opposite of success; it's a stepping stone toward it. I've learned this lesson deeply. My path was filled with early mistakes and tough moments, but I never saw them as defeat. Instead, I embraced them as learning opportunities. When I encountered roadblocks, I'd analyze them, adapt, and use the knowledge gained to move forward. Richard Branson's story of Virgin Cola and Virgin Cars failing didn't stop him from creating one of the world's most diverse business empires, and neither did my early setbacks stop me from continuing my journey.

**Overcoming the Fear of Failure:**

Reframe your thinking: Shift from "What if I fail?" to "What can I learn?"

Celebrate attempts: Recognize effort and progress, even if outcomes fall short.

**The Growth Mindset**

A growth mindset is the belief that abilities and intelligence can develop through effort and learning. This mindset is vital for entrepreneurs navigating evolving markets and technologies. Elon Musk's journey with SpaceX is a perfect example of this mindset. After three failed rocket launches nearly bankrupting the company, Musk and his team didn't give up. They used each failure to learn, refine, and eventually achieve the historic success of reusable rockets. Similarly, I've had to keep learning - whether it was upgrading my skills in web development, learning how to run a business, or managing teams. The path of an entrepreneur is about continuous learning and growth.

**Fostering a Growth Mindset:**

Seek feedback: Actively solicit constructive criticism and use it to improve.

Prioritize learning: Dedicate time to upskilling and staying updated on trends.

**Creativity and Innovation**

Innovation is the lifeblood of entrepreneurship. It requires the ability to look at problems from fresh angles, connecting disparate ideas, and devising unique solutions. My journey in web development has been all about finding innovative ways to deliver value to clients. I remember early on; I saw a gap in the market for affordable yet high-quality websites that could scale with businesses. This realization led me to craft solutions that were not only technically sound but also creatively designed to meet the evolving needs of our clients. It wasn't just about building websites - it was about offering digital experiences that transformed businesses.

**How to Enhance Creative Thinking:**

Engage in brainstorming: Regularly generate multiple ideas without judgment.

Cross-pollinate ideas: Explore concepts from different industries to inspire fresh approaches.

**Thriving Amid Uncertainty**

Entrepreneurship thrives in unpredictability. It's about making decisions with incomplete information and adapting to change. I learned this early on when I had to decide whether to take my business online in the face of fierce competition. It was a calculated risk, but I trusted in my ability to navigate the uncertainty and make it work. Today, DevelopUs.tech is a thriving business, and I attribute much of that success to my ability to adapt and stay flexible in the face of change.

**Practical Tips for Navigating Uncertainty:**

Focus on controllables: Prioritize actions within your influence.

Maintain agility: Be ready to pivot strategies as needed.

**Ethics and Impact**

Long-term success in entrepreneurship relies on trust and integrity. Entrepreneurs who prioritize ethical practices create lasting value. For me, building a business wasn't just about profit - it was about creating a brand that people could trust. Whether it's delivering high-quality work or treating my team with respect, I've always believed that maintaining integrity and staying true to my values is essential for sustainable success. It's this commitment to ethical practices that has helped DevelopUs.tech gain credibility and build long-term relationships with clients and partners alike.

**Actionable Insight:** Define your core values and ensure they guide your decisions.

**Conclusion: The Entrepreneurial Mindset in Action**

The entrepreneurial mindset is the foundation for navigating the unpredictable, ever-changing landscape of business. It's a blend of vision, resilience, creativity, adaptability, and ethics - traits that empower you to create innovative solutions, bounce back from setbacks, and continuously grow. These qualities have guided me throughout my journey, and as you read through this book, I hope you'll see how cultivating these traits can transform your journey as well. Each chapter will offer practical insights and strategies to help you hone this mindset and bring your entrepreneurial vision to life.

CHAPTER TWO

# Identifying Opportunities in a Changing Market

As we transition from understanding the entrepreneurial mindset discussed in the previous chapter, we now turn to a fundamental and transformative skill for every entrepreneur: the art of identifying opportunities in an ever-changing market. This skill is not merely about spotting the obvious but about delving deeper into the subtleties of change - recognizing unmet needs, anticipating shifts in consumer behavior, and seeing possibilities where others perceive only challenges.

Opportunities, like seeds, often hide in the fertile but overlooked soils of disruption and innovation. Some remain dormant until cultivated by visionaries who dare to think differently. The market is dynamic, constantly reshaped by economic forces, technological advancements, cultural changes, and unexpected global events. Entrepreneurs who learn to navigate this shifting landscape, not by fighting its currents but by harnessing its momentum, set themselves apart from the competition.

## The Foundations of Opportunity Identification

At its core, identifying opportunities is an exercise in observation and understanding. It requires both a structured approach - using tools and methodologies - and an unstructured openness to ideas and inspiration.

Historically, many groundbreaking businesses have been built on intuition and passion, but the modern world demands more. Today's entrepreneurs must pair their intuition with rigorous analysis and foresight. Market research, once a luxury, has become the cornerstone of this process. By deeply understanding markets, entrepreneurs move from reacting to change to anticipating it, positioning themselves as leaders rather than followers.

**The Importance of Market Research**

Market research is the bridge between imagination and execution. It takes the abstract - an idea, a vision - and anchors it in the tangible realities of consumer behavior, industry trends, and competitive landscapes. Entrepreneurs who excel in market research often uncover truths that others miss, seeing not just what the market wants but what it will need next.

Take the emergence of digital collaboration tools like Zoom, Slack, and Asana. These platforms didn't merely respond to a current need - they anticipated a world where remote work would become not just a trend but a necessity. They were prepared when the pandemic accelerated this shift, proving the value of foresight grounded in data.

**Techniques for Effective Market Research**

1. **Surveys and Focus Groups**: These traditional tools remain invaluable for understanding customer preferences. Asking the right questions and listening to nuanced answers often reveals opportunities hidden beneath surface-level feedback.

2. **Social Listening**: The rise of social media has created a treasure trove of consumer insights. By monitoring conversations, reviews, and trending topics, entrepreneurs can identify pain points and emerging needs.

3. **Competitor Analysis**: Understanding your competitors' strengths and weaknesses not only highlights market gaps but also ensures differentiation. Look at what they are doing well - and where they are falling short.

4. **Advanced Analytics**: Platforms like Google Trends and Tableau allow businesses to identify patterns that might not be immediately obvious. These tools convert raw data into actionable insights, helping entrepreneurs see where the market is heading.

Market research is not a one-and-done task; it is a continuous process, much like maintaining a compass to ensure you remain on course.

**Staying Ahead of Trends**

The modern entrepreneur lives in a world defined by rapid change. Technological advances, shifting cultural norms, and evolving consumer preferences can create opportunities as quickly as they render old methods obsolete. Staying ahead of these changes isn't just advantageous - it's essential.

**Recognizing Trends Before They Become Mainstream**

Trends often begin as faint signals, whispers in the noise of daily life. Entrepreneurs who learn to listen to these whispers can position themselves to ride the wave of change rather than be overwhelmed by it.

Take, for instance, the rise of plant-based diets. What began as a niche movement among environmentalists and health enthusiasts has grown into a multi-billion-dollar industry encompassing food products, restaurants, and even beauty products. Companies like Beyond Meat and Oatly identified this shift early, capitalizing on the growing demand for sustainable and ethical consumption.

**Practical Strategies for Trend Analysis**

- **Track Macro and Micro Trends**: Macro trends are broad shifts, such as the global push for sustainability. Micro trends are smaller, niche movements that often signal the direction of larger changes.
- **Monitor Adjacent Industries**: Innovation often happens at the intersections of industries. Entrepreneurs who look beyond their immediate field can uncover transformative ideas.
- **Engage with Thought Leaders**: Industry reports, podcasts, and blogs by leading thinkers provide valuable foresight into where markets are heading.

## The Art of Recognizing Unmet Needs

Consumer needs are the foundation of every successful business, but the most transformative ideas often address needs that consumers themselves don't yet recognize. This requires a deep level of empathy, creativity, and analytical thinking.

### Going Beyond the Obvious

On the surface, consumer complaints might seem straightforward: a product doesn't work as expected, or a service is too expensive. But entrepreneurs who look deeper often discover unmet needs that transcend these complaints.

Consider the example of the iPhone. Before its launch, consumers weren't clamouring for a device that combined a phone, camera, and internet browser in one sleek package. But Apple, through its deep understanding of how technology could integrate into daily life, created a product that fulfilled needs consumers didn't yet know they had.

### Spotting Market Disruptions

Disruptions are often viewed with trepidation, but for entrepreneurs, they are goldmines of opportunity. Whether it's a new technology, a regulatory shift, or a cultural change, disruptions redefine markets and create new spaces for innovation.

### Embracing Change as Opportunity

The ride-sharing industry, led by Uber and Lyft, exemplifies this. By leveraging mobile technology and addressing inefficiencies in traditional taxi services, these companies not only disrupted an industry but also created entirely new markets - for instance, food delivery through Uber Eats and DoorDash.

Disruptions force consumers to change their habits, and within that change lies opportunity. Entrepreneurs who can foresee how behaviors will adapt - and build solutions tailored to those adaptations - position themselves as pioneers.

## Case Studies: Entrepreneurs Who Saw the Future

### Spotify

Recognizing the transition from music ownership to access, Spotify introduced a streaming platform that offered personalized playlists, a freemium model, and an easy-to-use interface. Today, it dominates the music streaming market.

### Teladoc Health

As remote communication technologies improved, Teladoc saw an opportunity in telemedicine. By offering virtual consultations, they transformed the healthcare landscape, especially during the COVID-19 pandemic.

### Airbnb

By recognizing the growing appeal of authentic, local travel experiences, Airbnb disrupted the hospitality industry, creating a platform that empowered homeowners while meeting traveller's desires for unique stays.

## Conclusion: The Future Belongs to the Observant

The skill of identifying opportunities is a blend of art and science. It requires both an analytical mind and a creative spirit, a willingness to listen and the courage to act. As you refine your ability to see what others miss, remember that opportunities often lie at the intersection of change and vision.

In the next chapter, we'll explore how to craft a unique value proposition - turning these opportunities into compelling offers that capture the hearts and minds of your audience. For now, take this truth to heart: markets are ever-changing, but the entrepreneurial spirit thrives on change.

CHAPTER THREE

# Crafting your Unique Value Proposition

*"In a world full of choices, your unique value proposition is what makes you the first choice."*

***– Mr. Rohan Kumar Bhoi***

Every successful business begins with a clear and compelling vision, but beyond the dream lies the core element that will set you apart from your competitors: your **Unique Value Proposition (UVP)**. The UVP is not merely a catchy slogan, nor is it a list of features you offer. It's the essence of what your brand promises and the compelling reason why a customer should choose you over anyone else.

As entrepreneurs, the task of creating a UVP is one of the most critical and foundational steps in building a thriving business. A well-crafted UVP can provide clarity, drive customer loyalty, and attract your ideal clients. In a market crowded with choices, your UVP is the beacon that guides customers to your doorstep. It's your opportunity to communicate what makes your product or service not only necessary but irreplaceable.

**The Core of Your Value Proposition**

Your UVP is more than a marketing message; it's the heart of your business strategy. It begins with one critical question: *What makes your offering irreplaceable?*

Think of the legendary companies that have redefined industries through their unique propositions. Tesla, for example, didn't just build electric cars. They revolutionized transportation by combining cutting-edge technology with sustainability, offering an alternative to traditional vehicles while accelerating the world's transition to clean energy. Tesla's UVP wasn't just about making electric cars - it was about shaping the future of the planet.

Similarly, when I founded DevelopUs.tech, the core of our value proposition lay not just in delivering web development services but in offering **tailored digital solutions** that were not only functional but also transformative for our clients. Our ability to integrate innovation with excellence was at the heart of our brand, making us irreplaceable in the eyes of our customers.

To truly understand what makes your product or service irreplaceable, start by diving deep into three key areas:

1. **The Problem You Solve**
   Every great business solves a problem. Understanding the problem your product or service addresses is the foundation of your UVP. Whether you're simplifying a complex task, offering convenience, or alleviating pain points, your UVP must articulate the problem and position your brand as the best solution.

2. **How You Solve It**
   The next step is to evaluate how your offering solves this problem better than anything else on the market. Do you offer better quality, more affordability, faster delivery, or a unique experience? Defining what sets you apart - your competitive edge - is key to crafting a value proposition that speaks to your customers' needs.

3. **What Makes You Unique**
   The final piece of the puzzle is to establish what truly differentiates your brand. This is where innovation often comes into play. What can you offer that your competitors don't? Whether it's your product design, customer service, or a pioneering approach, this uniqueness is the lifeblood of your UVP.

**The Sweet Spot: Where Passion, Skill, and Market Needs Meet**

Creating a UVP isn't just about what you can do - it's about what you *must* do. It's about discovering the sweet spot where your passion intersects with what you're good at and what the market demands.

This process begins with introspection. Ask yourself:

- **What drives you?**
- **What do you excel at?**
- **What does the market need that isn't being fully met?**

For example, consider the story of Sara Blakely, the founder of Spanx. She identified a gap in the market for comfortable, slimming undergarments, a need that many consumers weren't fully aware of. By focusing on solving this discomfort and providing women with confidence, she not only created a product but built an entirely new category in the apparel industry. Spanx's UVP wasn't just about creating shapewear - it was about empowering women to feel confident, comfortable, and supported. This approach, combined with innovative product design, led to the creation of a billion-dollar company.

Similarly, when I established DevelopUs.tech, my passion for technology and digital design intersected with the growing demand for businesses to have an online presence. I realized that there was a gap between businesses needing quality digital solutions and the available offerings in the market. We set out to create not just websites, but personalized, **innovative digital experiences** that transformed our clients' businesses.

**Communicating Your UVP in a Crowded Market**

Once you've defined your UVP, the next step is communication. In a crowded marketplace, it's not enough to simply know what makes your business special - you must also communicate it effectively to your customers. This is where the art of storytelling becomes invaluable.

Humans are inherently drawn to stories. A compelling narrative can elevate your UVP from a simple statement to a message that resonates on a deeper level with your audience. Take **TOMS Shoes**, for example. Their UVP wasn't just about selling shoes; it was about creating a movement. TOMS' "One for One" model - where each pair of shoes purchased meant a pair donated to a child in need - created an emotional connection with consumers. This powerful story turned TOMS into more than a shoe company; it became a brand that represented kindness and social responsibility.

When crafting your own narrative, think beyond features and benefits. Focus on the **why** behind your offering. Why did you start your business? What change do you hope to make in the world? Why should customers care?

For DevelopUs.tech, the story we shared with our clients wasn't just about our technical expertise; it was about our commitment to delivering personalized solutions that transformed their businesses. We didn't just build websites; we created digital assets that helped our clients achieve their goals. This message resonated with customers and differentiated us in an overcrowded market.

**Innovation: Carving Your Niche**

One of the most powerful ways to differentiate your offering is through innovation. Innovation is not always about creating something entirely new - it can also be about offering a new perspective on an existing product or service.

Consider the example of **Warby Parker**, which disrupted the eyewear industry. Their value proposition wasn't merely about selling glasses; it was about offering high-quality, designer glasses at an affordable price. By cutting out the middleman and selling directly to consumers, Warby Parker revolutionized the eyewear market, making stylish and affordable glasses accessible to a broader audience. They also implemented a socially conscious element with their "Buy a Pair, give a Pair" program, further enhancing their UVP.

Similarly, **Beyond Meat** transformed the food industry by offering a plant-based protein alternative that mimicked the taste and texture of real meat. Beyond Meat's value proposition wasn't just about offering a vegetarian option - it was about creating a healthier, more sustainable alternative for meat-eaters and vegetarians alike. This innovation helped Beyond Meat stand out in the competitive food industry, appealing to a wide customer base.

Innovation often comes from a **deep understanding of unmet needs** in the market. The best entrepreneurs are the ones who see the world differently and create solutions that others hadn't yet imagined.

### Adapting Your UVP Over Time

A UVP isn't a static element of your business - it must evolve as markets change, customer preferences shift, and new opportunities arise. Companies that have stood the test of time, such as **Netflix**, have done so by adapting their value propositions to remain relevant.

Netflix started with a simple value proposition of DVD rentals by mail. They eliminated late fees and offered convenience, but as streaming technology became more accessible, Netflix evolved. Today, their UVP centers around providing unlimited access to a vast library of high-quality content, including original programming, all on-demand. Their ability to pivot and adapt to changes in the industry kept them ahead of the competition.

This adaptability is crucial for any entrepreneur. Your UVP must evolve with your business, staying in tune with changes in the marketplace while remaining true to your core values.

### Conclusion: Standing Out in a Crowded Market

In a world that's constantly evolving and filled with competition, your UVP is the guiding light that keeps your business on track. It's your promise to your customers that you will solve their problems in a way that no one else can.

By taking the time to define what makes your product irreplaceable, communicate that value effectively, and innovate to carve out a unique niche, you will set yourself up for long-term success. Your UVP is the bedrock upon which your business is built. It will guide your decisions, shape your brand, and help you stand out in an overcrowded marketplace.

As we move forward to the next chapter, we'll explore how to build a team that can bring your UVP to life, helping you scale and drive the success of your business. Together, we'll take the steps necessary to make your vision a reality.

CHAPTER FOUR

# Strategic Decision Making

As entrepreneurs, we often find ourselves at crossroads, facing decisions that can shape the future of our businesses. These decisions, whether big or small, define the direction of our ventures. While some choices seem intuitive, others demand careful analysis and structured thinking. Strategic decision-making is the backbone of successful entrepreneurship, and mastering this skill is essential for long-term success.

Entrepreneurship, by its nature, is fraught with uncertainty. Unlike established corporations that can rely on years of data and historical precedent, startups are often navigating uncharted waters. This constant state of flux means that entrepreneurs must be prepared to make decisions quickly and effectively, often with limited information. The ability to make sound choices under such conditions is not only crucial but can be the differentiating factor between those who succeed and those who falter.

In this chapter, we will explore how strategic decision-making frameworks can help entrepreneurs make the best possible choices in uncertain environments. We will also discuss the delicate balance between intuition and data, and the importance of both in making critical decisions. Finally, we'll examine real-world examples of tough calls made by successful entrepreneurs and draw lessons from their experiences.

## Decision-Making Frameworks for Uncertainty and Rapid Change

The business world is dynamic, and the pace of change is only accelerating. To keep up with this ever-evolving landscape, entrepreneurs need to be agile decision-makers, capable of adapting their strategies on the fly. One of the most powerful tools at an entrepreneur's disposal is a **decision-making framework**. These frameworks offer structured approaches to decision-making, helping entrepreneurs process information, weigh options, and make choices with confidence.

### The OODA Loop: Observe, Orient, Decide, Act

One of the most effective decision-making frameworks, particularly in uncertain and rapidly changing environments, is the **OODA Loop**. Originally developed by military strategist John Boyd, the OODA Loop is designed to help individuals and organizations make decisions quickly, adjust strategies, and stay ahead of competitors.

**Observe:** The first step in the OODA Loop is to observe the environment. This involves gathering relevant data, monitoring market conditions, and staying aware of both internal and external factors that may impact the decision.

**Orient:** In this stage, entrepreneurs analyze the information gathered and align it with their objectives. This step involves critical thinking, questioning assumptions, and evaluating how different variables may affect the decision at hand.

**Decide:** After orienting themselves, entrepreneurs make a decision. This may be a quick, instinctive choice or one based on careful deliberation. The key here is to move decisively rather than becoming paralyzed by uncertainty.

**Act:** The final step is to take action. This involves implementing the decision and monitoring its impact. Entrepreneurs must be prepared to iterate and adapt if the results of their decision require adjustments.

The OODA Loop is particularly beneficial for entrepreneurs in high-stakes environments where speed and adaptability are critical. By following this iterative process, entrepreneurs can maintain a proactive approach to decision-making, ensuring they stay ahead of the competition.

### The Eisenhower Matrix: Prioritizing Decisions

Another useful framework for entrepreneurs is the **Eisenhower Matrix**, which helps prioritize tasks and decisions based on their urgency and importance. By categorizing decisions into four quadrants, entrepreneurs can focus their energy on what truly matters:

1. **Urgent and Important:** These are the decisions that demand immediate attention and are critical to the business's success. Entrepreneurs should prioritize these decisions and address them as soon as possible.
2. **Important but Not Urgent:** These decisions are significant but don't require immediate action. Entrepreneurs should allocate time and resources to these decisions to ensure long-term success.
3. **Urgent but Not Important:** These decisions may seem pressing, but they don't have a significant impact on the business. Entrepreneurs should delegate or minimize time spent on these tasks.
4. **Neither Urgent Nor Important:** These decisions can often be deferred or eliminated altogether.

By using the Eisenhower Matrix, entrepreneurs can gain clarity on where to focus their efforts, preventing distractions and ensuring they are making decisions that align with their long-term goals.

### Scenario Planning: Preparing for the Unknown

Finally, **scenario planning** is an essential tool for entrepreneurs navigating uncertain times. Scenario planning involves creating multiple possible future scenarios and developing strategies for each. This proactive approach allows entrepreneurs to prepare for various outcomes and reduce the impact of unforeseen events. Whether it's a new competitor entering the market or an economic downturn, scenario planning helps entrepreneurs maintain flexibility and stay prepared for any situation.

### Balancing Intuition and Data in Decision-Making

While decision-making frameworks provide structure and clarity, it's essential to recognize the role of intuition in the entrepreneurial process. Many successful entrepreneurs credit their intuition as a key driver of their decision-making. This "gut feeling" often emerges from years of experience, industry knowledge, and a deep understanding of customer needs. However, while intuition can be a valuable tool, it should not be the sole basis for critical decisions.

### The Role of Intuition in Entrepreneurship

Intuition in entrepreneurship is often described as a sixth sense - a deep understanding of market trends or customer behavior that goes beyond rational analysis. This type of insight is typically developed over time and with experience. For example, as an entrepreneur, my intuition often guided my early decisions when I founded **DevelopUs.tech**. I sensed that businesses were increasingly looking for customized digital solutions rather than generic products, even when data wasn't readily available to support this notion.

However, intuition should never be used in isolation, particularly when stakes are high. Relying solely on gut feeling can lead to biases and blind spots. It's essential to balance intuition with careful analysis and data-driven decision-making.

### The Power of Data-Driven Decisions

In today's data-rich world, the ability to collect, analyze, and interpret data has become a critical skill for entrepreneurs. Data-driven decision-making allows entrepreneurs to make informed choices based on facts rather than assumptions. This is especially important in industries where rapid change is the norm, such as technology and e-commerce.

For instance, A/B testing is a widely used method to test hypotheses and measure outcomes before making significant decisions.

Companies like **Facebook**, **Google**, and **Amazon** rely heavily on A/B testing to optimize user experiences, marketing strategies, and product features. By testing different versions of a product or campaign, entrepreneurs can gather real-world data to guide their decisions and minimize risk.

At the same time, entrepreneurs must recognize the limitations of data. Not all decisions can be quantified, and relying too heavily on data can sometimes obscure the broader vision. The key is to combine data with intuition, using both to inform decisions and adapt quickly.

### Examples of Tough Calls Made by Successful Entrepreneurs

To truly understand the impact of strategic decision-making, let's look at a few real-world examples of tough calls made by successful entrepreneurs. These decisions, while risky at the time, ultimately shaped the trajectory of their companies and industries.

### Reed Hastings and the Netflix Pivot to Streaming

In 2007, **Reed Hastings**, co-founder and CEO of Netflix, made a bold decision that would alter the entertainment landscape forever. At the time, Netflix was a successful DVD rental service, but Hastings recognized the potential of streaming video over the internet. Despite resistance from investors and skepticism from industry analysts, he made the decision to pivot Netflix towards streaming.

This move, which combined data analysis of internet trends and consumer behavior with Hastings' forward-thinking intuition, transformed Netflix into the dominant force in the entertainment industry. Today, Netflix's success in streaming video is a testament to the power of making bold decisions based on a blend of data, experience, and instinct.

### Howard Schultz and the Starbucks Reinvention

In 2008, **Howard Schultz**, then CEO of Starbucks, faced a critical decision in the wake of declining sales. Schultz made the controversial move to close all 7,100 Starbucks stores in the United States for three hours to retrain baristas on the art of making the perfect espresso. This decision, which cost the company an estimated $6 million in lost sales, was a calculated risk aimed at reinvigorating the brand and refocusing on quality.

At the time, many criticized Schultz for his decision, but in retrospect, it was a turning point in Starbucks' history. Schultz's willingness to make tough decisions, even at the risk of short-term losses, ensured that Starbucks maintained its commitment to quality and customer experience - a move that paid off in the long run.

**Elon Musk and Tesla's Risky Bet on Electric Vehicles**

When **Elon Musk** founded Tesla, the idea of electric vehicles (EVs) was still considered niche, and the technology was far from mainstream. Despite this, Musk made the risky decision to invest heavily in EV production, even though traditional car manufacturers were skeptical of the market's potential. His bold vision for sustainable transportation, backed by data-driven research and intuition about future trends, turned Tesla into the world's leading electric vehicle manufacturer.

Musk's willingness to challenge conventional wisdom, along with his ability to back up his decisions with rigorous analysis, reshaped the entire automotive industry.

**Conclusion: The Art and Science of Strategic Decision-Making**

Strategic decision-making is not a one-size-fits-all process. Entrepreneurs must develop their own decision-making style, informed by a combination of frameworks, data, intuition, and experience. The key to success lies in the ability to navigate uncertainty, make informed decisions quickly, and adjust strategies as needed.

As you move forward in your entrepreneurial journey, remember that every decision you make - whether big or small - shapes the trajectory of your business. Trust in your judgment, use the tools available to you, and never be afraid to make bold, calculated moves when the time is right.

In the next chapter, we will explore another crucial aspect of entrepreneurship: financial literacy. Understanding the numbers behind your business is essential for making informed decisions and ensuring long-term sustainability. We will delve into managing cash flow, evaluating funding options, and learning from startups that have mastered the art of financial management.

CHAPTER FIVE

# Financial Literacy for Entrepreneurs

As we move from the strategic decision-making processes explored in the previous chapter, we now turn our attention to a critical pillar of entrepreneurial success: **financial literacy**. The ability to understand, manage, and leverage financial resources is often the difference between a thriving business and one that falters. This chapter will provide you with essential financial knowledge and tools necessary to navigate the complex and ever-changing monetary landscape of entrepreneurship.

For many entrepreneurs, finances are an area of discomfort. But embracing financial literacy is not just about balancing books or understanding spreadsheets - it's about empowering yourself to make confident, informed decisions that will shape the future of your business. Mastering key concepts such as cash flow, profit margins, and investments lays the foundation for financial resilience. These principles will guide you as you make crucial decisions about funding options, investments, and the long-term sustainability of your business.

**Managing Cash Flow: The Lifeblood of Your Business**

Cash flow is perhaps the most vital financial aspect of any business. It represents the movement of money in and out of your company, ensuring that you have enough liquid assets to meet operational needs, such as paying employees, suppliers, and overheads. Yet, it is a concept that many entrepreneurs overlook, often to their detriment. A business can be profitable on paper but still face financial ruin if it doesn't manage cash flow effectively.

Cash flow is like the lifeblood of your business; without it, your operations grind to a halt. Positive cash flow enables you to reinvest in your business, pay down debt, return money to shareholders, and build financial security. Negative cash flow, on the other hand, indicates a decrease in your company's liquidity, which could signal the onset of financial trouble.

**Understanding and Managing Cash Flow**

To manage cash flow effectively, you must understand its components. Cash flow comes from both operations (revenue from customers) and financing activities (loans, investments). You should focus on ensuring that your incoming cash is greater than your outgoing cash, even if your business is not yet profitable. Cash management involves balancing income and expenses, optimizing receivables (the money your customers owe), and carefully controlling outflows (your expenses).

A crucial aspect of managing cash flow is forecasting. Predicting your future cash needs is a skill that every entrepreneur must develop. This includes projecting when you will receive payments from clients, when bills are due, and understanding your cash reserves.

**Example: Tesla's Cash Flow Crisis and Recovery**

A classic example of a company that faced significant cash flow challenges is **Tesla**. Despite its groundbreaking technology and vision, Tesla's financial situation was precarious for many years. In 2017, the company was burning through nearly $8,000 per minute. The pressure was immense as the company struggled to meet production deadlines and pay its suppliers. However, through meticulous management, including optimizing production efficiency, reducing costs, and securing strategic partnerships, Tesla turned its cash flow positive by the third quarter of 2018. This turnaround highlights the critical importance of understanding cash flow and how strategic financial management can prevent a company from collapsing under financial strain.

## Profit Margins: Turning Revenue into Sustainable Profit

Profit margin is another foundational metric that entrepreneurs must grasp. It represents the percentage of revenue that translates into profit after accounting for all expenses. Profit margins are a vital indicator of your company's financial health and sustainability.

There are two main types of profit margins to be aware of:

1. **Gross Profit Margin**: This is calculated by subtracting the direct costs associated with producing goods or services (cost of goods sold, or COGS) from your revenue, then dividing that by your total revenue. It gives insight into how efficiently your company is producing and selling its offerings.
2. **Net Profit Margin**: This is the most comprehensive measure, accounting for all expenses, including operating costs, interest, taxes, and depreciation. A healthy net profit margin indicates that your business is not only making sales but also efficiently converting those sales into profit.

### Optimizing Profit Margins

Optimizing your profit margins requires balancing pricing strategies, cost management, and operational efficiencies. Entrepreneurs often focus solely on increasing sales, but the real key to profitability lies in maximizing the amount of profit each sale generates.

### Example: Warby Parker's Disruption of the Eyewear Industry

Consider **Warby Parker**, an eyewear company that disrupted the industry by offering high-quality, designer glasses at a fraction of the price of traditional retailers. The company achieved this by cutting out the middlemen and selling directly to consumers online. This allowed Warby Parker to maintain healthy profit margins while offering affordable prices to customers. Their ability to manage their costs while providing significant value to consumers set the stage for their rapid growth and success in the marketplace.

By optimizing their profit margins, Warby Parker not only became a profitable business but also found ways to reinvest in social causes, further strengthening their brand and customer loyalty.

**Investments: Making Strategic Financial Decisions**

Investments are one of the most crucial decisions that entrepreneurs will face. Whether investing in equipment, technology, marketing, or talent, these decisions directly affect your business's ability to grow and remain competitive.

Understanding how to evaluate potential investments critically is key. A well-thought-out investment strategy considers both short-term costs and long-term benefits, and involves analyzing metrics like **Return on Investment (ROI)**, **Payback Periods**, and **Opportunity Costs**. The goal is to ensure that the capital you deploy generates value that exceeds its initial cost.

**Long-Term Investment Thinking**

Consider **Amazon** and its early investments in fulfillment centers. When Jeff Bezos started Amazon, he faced skepticism from analysts who viewed these massive investments as detrimental to the company's short-term profits. However, Bezos was focused on long-term growth, believing that creating an efficient distribution system would allow Amazon to scale rapidly and provide superior service to customers. Today, Amazon's fulfillment centers are a cornerstone of its business, contributing significantly to its position as the e-commerce leader. Bezos' ability to invest in infrastructure early on - despite pressure for immediate profitability - was a key factor in Amazon's long-term success.

**Choosing the Right Funding Option: Bootstrapping, Venture Capital, or Loans**

As you grow your business, you will likely face the critical decision of how to fund that growth. Each option - **bootstrapping**, **venture capital**, or **loans** - comes with its own advantages and challenges, and your choice will have significant implications for the future direction of your company.

### Bootstrapping: Maintaining Control and Financial Discipline

Bootstrapping is when entrepreneurs fund their businesses using personal savings or revenue generated from operations. This approach offers the advantage of maintaining full control over the business, as no external investors are involved. However, bootstrapping also places significant financial pressure on the founder and may limit the company's ability to scale rapidly.

### Example: Mailchimp's Success through Bootstrapping

One remarkable example of bootstrapping success is **Mailchimp**, the email marketing platform. Founded in 2001, Mailchimp grew organically for 17 years without taking any outside investment. By 2018, it had reached $600 million in revenue and was valued at $4.2 billion. The founders, Ben Chestnut and Dan Kurzius, were able to maintain complete control over the company's direction, creating a unique product and company culture without the pressure of external investors demanding rapid growth.

### Venture Capital: Fuel for Rapid Growth

On the other hand, **venture capital** can provide significant funding that allows a company to scale quickly, access valuable expertise, and expand into new markets. However, it also means giving up some degree of ownership and control over the company.

### Example: Airbnb's Journey with Venture Capital

The journey of **Airbnb** offers valuable lessons in how venture capital can both propel and complicate a company's growth. Early on, Airbnb struggled to attract investors, with many dismissing its model as too risky. However, after securing initial funding from Y Combinator, Airbnb went on to raise multiple rounds of venture capital, which allowed it to grow rapidly and scale internationally. Despite this success, the founders had to balance their vision with the expectations of investors seeking high returns, making strategic decisions that aligned with both short-term financial needs and long-term goals.

### Loans: Borrowing for Stability and Control

Finally, **loans** offer a middle ground between bootstrapping and equity funding. Loans allow entrepreneurs to access capital without diluting ownership, but they come with the obligation to repay with interest. For many businesses, loans can be an effective way to manage cash flow or fund specific growth initiatives.

### Example: Honest Tea's Strategic Use of Loans

**Honest Tea**, the organic beverage company, provides an example of using loans to fuel growth. Founder **Seth Goldman** utilized a combination of personal savings, loans from friends and family, and a line of credit from a local bank to fund the company's early years. This strategy allowed Honest Tea to expand gradually while maintaining its independence, eventually attracting the attention of **Coca-Cola**, leading to a successful acquisition.

### Financial Resilience: Navigating Challenges with Strategic Planning

Entrepreneurial financial resilience is the ability to adapt to unexpected challenges, market downturns, or rapid growth without compromising the long-term health of your business. Building financial resilience requires careful planning, maintaining adequate cash reserves, and having contingency plans in place.

### Example: Airbnb's Response to the COVID-19 Pandemic

Airbnb's response to the COVID-19 pandemic illustrates the importance of financial resilience. When global travel ground to a halt in early 2020, Airbnb's business was severely impacted. However, the company's strong cash position and ability to quickly reduce costs allowed it to survive the initial shock. More importantly, Airbnb pivoted its business model to focus on long-term stays and local travel experiences, a move that not only helped the company weather the crisis but positioned it for a successful IPO later that year.

**Conclusion: Financial Mastery for Entrepreneurial Success**

As we conclude this chapter on financial literacy, remember that mastering these concepts is an ongoing process. The financial landscape is constantly evolving, with new funding models, changing regulations, and emerging technologies reshaping the field. Successful entrepreneurs commit to lifelong learning, staying informed about financial trends and continuously refining their strategies to adapt to the changing environment.

In the next chapter, we will explore the crucial topic of **building a sustainable business model**. As you'll see, the financial literacy skills discussed here form the foundation for creating a business that thrives in the long term, adapts to market changes, and delivers value to customers and stakeholders alike. Financial acumen, combined with strategic vision, creates the potential for transformative entrepreneurship.

CHAPTER SIX

# Building a Sustainable Business Model

The journey of entrepreneurship is often marked by high ambitions, unforeseen challenges, and a constant push to create something of enduring value. Among all the hurdles an entrepreneur faces, none is more critical than constructing a **sustainable business model**. A business model is not merely a blueprint for profitability; it's a dynamic framework that adapts, evolves, and stands resilient against the tests of time and change.

In this chapter, we delve deep into the art and science of building such a model - one that aligns with long-term objectives, embraces adaptability, and ensures consistent value creation for customers, stakeholders, and society at large.

**Why Sustainability Matters in a Business Model**

A sustainable business model is the backbone of any successful enterprise. It goes beyond the immediate goal of revenue generation to address critical questions:

- How will your business remain relevant as market conditions shift?
- How can your processes and strategies evolve to meet the needs of tomorrow's customers?
- How do you balance growth with responsibility - both social and environmental?

Sustainability is about creating a business that not only survives but thrives. It's a commitment to being agile in strategy and unwavering in purpose.

**The Evolution of Market Expectations**

Today's customers demand more than just a product or service; they seek experiences, transparency, and values that resonate with their own. A sustainable model integrates these expectations, ensuring your business remains a trusted partner in their journey.

**Adaptability: The Cornerstone of Resilience**

In an age of disruption, the ability to adapt can mean the difference between survival and extinction. A rigid business model may work in a predictable environment, but in today's volatile markets, adaptability is not a luxury; it's a necessity.

**Case Study: Netflix - A Masterclass in Adaptability**

Netflix's story is a testament to the power of adaptability. Founded in 1997 as a DVD rental service, the company faced declining demand for physical media as streaming technology gained traction. Rather than clinging to its original business model, Netflix pivoted to embrace digital streaming, revolutionizing how people consume entertainment.

But the transformation didn't stop there. Anticipating the need for original content, Netflix invested heavily in production, creating critically acclaimed shows and movies that solidified its position as an industry leader.

This adaptability underscores a vital lesson: success lies not in rigidly adhering to your initial vision but in recognizing opportunities and having the courage to pivot when necessary.

**The Iterative Nature of a Sustainable Model**

A sustainable business model is never static. It evolves through constant evaluation, feedback, and refinement. This iterative process ensures your business remains aligned with market needs and is prepared to seize new opportunities.

### Tools for Iteration: The Business Model Canvas

One effective method for evaluating and refining your model is the **Business Model Canvas**, developed by Alexander Osterwalder and Yves Pigneur. This framework divides a business into nine critical components:

**Customer Segments**: Who are you serving?

**Value Propositions**: What unique value do you deliver?

**Channels**: How do you reach your customers?

**Customer Relationships**: How do you interact with and retain customers?

**Revenue Streams**: How do you make money?

**Key Resources**: What assets are essential for your business?

**Key Activities**: What are the most important actions your business must take?

**Key Partnerships**: Who are your strategic allies?

**Cost Structure**: What are your major costs?

By revisiting and updating this canvas regularly, you ensure that your model adapts to changes in customer behavior, technological advancements, and competitive pressures.

### Learning from Industry Pivots

Some of the most enduring companies owe their success to well-timed pivots - transformations that redefined their purpose and repositioned them for sustained growth.

### Slack: From Gaming to Productivity Powerhouse

Originally conceived as a gaming company, Slack's founders noticed the inefficiency of existing team communication tools. They decided to pivot, repurposing their internal tool into what we now know as Slack - a transformative workplace communication platform. This bold shift turned a failing game studio into a multibillion-dollar enterprise.

**Instagram: Simplifying to Succeed**

Instagram began as Burbn, a location-based app with numerous features. When the founder's realized users were primarily engaging with its photo-sharing feature, they stripped away all other functionalities and rebranded as Instagram. This streamlined focus propelled the app to global success, leading to its acquisition by Facebook for $1 billion.

These stories highlight the importance of staying attuned to market signals and being willing to redefine your business when opportunities arise.

**Balancing Consistency and Flexibility**

While adaptability is crucial, constant change can dilute your brand and confuse customers. The art lies in striking the right balance - remaining true to your core mission while being flexible in your approach.

**Scenario Planning: Preparing for the Future**

One effective way to maintain this balance is through **scenario planning**. This involves envisioning multiple future scenarios for your industry and designing strategies to navigate each one. By anticipating changes, you can position your business to respond effectively without compromising its identity.

**Sustainability as a Value Driver**

Sustainability is not just a buzzword; it's a strategic advantage. Companies that prioritize sustainable practices often enjoy stronger customer loyalty, better employee engagement, and long-term profitability.

### Case Study: Patagonia - Leading with Purpose

Patagonia has built its brand on environmental sustainability, from using recycled materials to encouraging customers to repair rather than replace products. This commitment has fostered a loyal customer base and positioned Patagonia as a leader in responsible business practices.

### Embedding Innovation in Your Model

A truly sustainable business model fosters a culture of innovation. Encourage your team to challenge the status quo, experiment with new ideas, and view failures as opportunities to learn.

### Key Strategies for Innovation

**Empower Teams**: Give employees the freedom to propose and test new ideas.

**Collaborate Externally**: Partner with startups, research institutions, or even competitors to drive innovation.

**Invest in Technology**: Leverage emerging technologies to streamline operations and create new revenue streams.

### Conclusion: A Model for the Future

Building a sustainable business model is not a one-time achievement but an ongoing process of evolution and adaptation. By embracing feedback, staying agile, and fostering innovation, you can create a framework that not only meets today's challenges but also anticipates tomorrow's opportunities.

In the next chapter, we will explore how to translate the principles of a sustainable business model into a compelling **marketing and branding strategy**. After all, a great business model is only as effective as your ability to communicate its value to the world.

CHAPTER SEVEN

# Marketing and Branding in the Digital Age

The digital age has revolutionized how businesses communicate, engage, and build relationships with their customers. For entrepreneurs, this transformation has opened unparalleled opportunities to connect with their target audience, shape perceptions, and establish a strong brand presence. Yet, it has also introduced complexities that require a deeper understanding of the digital landscape.

In this chapter, we delve into the art and science of marketing and branding in the modern world, exploring how storytelling can foster emotional connections, how social media becomes a bridge between brands and audiences, and how data and technology are essential tools for creating impactful campaigns. For any business aspiring to succeed in this digital-first era, mastering these elements is not optional - it is vital.

**The Power of Storytelling in Shaping Brands**

At the heart of every memorable brand lies a compelling story. Storytelling is a timeless art, but its importance in modern branding cannot be overstated. In an era where attention spans are fleeting and competition is relentless, stories provide a way to connect with customers on a deeper, emotional level. A well-crafted narrative has the power to humanize your brand, making it more relatable and memorable.

Take the example of Airbnb, a company that began as a simple platform for renting out spare rooms. Its "Belong Anywhere" campaign transformed the brand's image, emphasizing not just places to stay but the meaningful experiences and connections that travel enables. This shift in narrative allowed Airbnb to redefine its market positioning, resonating with travellers seeking authenticity and community. The stories of real hosts and guests became a cornerstone of their branding strategy, fostering trust and a sense of belonging among its users.

A brand story, however, must be authentic. Customers today are discerning; they can quickly detect when a narrative feels forced or insincere. The essence of a brand's story should stem from its mission, values, and the unique journey of its founders. For example, if your business was born out of a personal struggle to solve a problem, sharing that experience can inspire and connect with others facing similar challenges.

**Social Media: The Digital Marketplace for Connections**

Social media has become the beating heart of digital marketing - a vibrant space where brands and customers interact in real time. But the true power of social media lies not in its reach but in its ability to create genuine connections. For brands, this means moving beyond merely broadcasting messages to actively engaging with their audience.

The beauty of social media lies in its diversity of platforms, each with its own unique characteristics. Instagram thrives on visual storytelling, while LinkedIn caters to professional discourse. Twitter is the home of brevity and wit, while TikTok is redefining content consumption with its short, dynamic videos. Choosing the right platform is not just about where your audience is most active, but also about aligning with your brand's voice and objectives.

Consider the rise of Glossier, a beauty brand that built its empire on the foundations of social media. Glossier didn't just market its products; it created a community. By involving customers in product development and amplifying their voices on social media, Glossier fostered a sense of ownership and loyalty. This customer-centric approach turned ordinary consumers into brand ambassadors, creating a powerful word-of-mouth engine that propelled the brand's growth.

Yet, social media success is not solely about engagement; it's also about consistency and authenticity. Every post, comment, and campaign should reflect the core values of your brand. It's in this consistency that brands build trust, turning followers into lifelong customers.

**Content Creation: The Soul of Digital Marketing**

Content creation is the lifeblood of any digital marketing strategy. It is through content - whether in the form of blogs, videos, podcasts, or infographics - that brands communicate their value, educate their audience, and establish authority in their niche.

However, creating impactful content requires a balance between creativity and strategy. The content must be high quality, relevant, and aligned with the preferences of your audience. Quantity without quality often leads to diminishing returns, as audiences today value meaningful and engaging content over mindless noise.

A masterclass in content marketing can be seen in the viral launch of Dollar Shave Club. Their humorous and unapologetically candid video, "Our Blades Are F***ing Great," perfectly captured the essence of their brand while delivering their value proposition in an entertaining manner. The video not only resonated with their target audience but also established Dollar Shave Club as a disruptor in the grooming industry.

Content must evolve alongside consumer behavior. The rise of video content, particularly short-form formats like Instagram Reels and TikTok videos, underscores the importance of adapting to changing consumption patterns. Brands that can deliver concise, visually engaging content have a significant advantage in capturing attention in an oversaturated digital market.

**Data: The Compass for Digital Marketing**

In the digital world, data is not just a tool - it's a compass guiding every decision. The availability of real-time analytics has transformed marketing from a creative discipline into a science. Every click, view, and interaction can be measured, offering invaluable insights into customer behavior and campaign performance.

For instance, A/B testing allows businesses to experiment with different strategies to identify what resonates most with their audience. By testing variables such as headlines, visuals, and call-to-action buttons, brands can optimize their campaigns for maximum impact.

Consider how Sephora, a global beauty brand, leverages customer data to personalize the shopping experience. By analyzing purchase history and browsing behavior, Sephora tailors product recommendations and marketing messages to individual preferences. This data-driven approach not only enhances the customer experience but also drives higher conversion rates.

However, data usage comes with responsibility. As consumers become more aware of data privacy, brands must prioritize transparency and ethical practices. Establishing trust in how customer data is handled can differentiate your brand and foster long-term loyalty.

**Embracing Trends and Emerging Technologies**

The digital landscape is ever-changing, with new trends and technologies continuously reshaping how brands interact with their audience. Staying ahead of these changes is crucial for maintaining relevance.

Voice search, for example, is becoming a significant factor in SEO strategy. With the proliferation of voice-activated devices like Alexa and Google Home, optimizing content for natural, conversational language is no longer optional. Similarly, augmented reality (AR) and virtual reality (VR) are opening new possibilities for immersive brand experiences.

A standout example is IKEA's AR app, which allows customers to visualize furniture in their homes before making a purchase. This innovative approach not only enhances the shopping experience but also builds trust by helping customers make informed decisions.

**The Essence of Marketing in the Digital Age**

Marketing and branding in the digital age are both a challenge and an opportunity. While the tools and platforms have evolved, the core principles remain unchanged: authenticity, value, and meaningful connection. A brand that consistently tells its story, engages its audience, and adapts to change will not just survive in this competitive landscape - it will thrive.

As we move to the next chapter, which explores the role of technology in driving growth, remember that the ultimate goal of marketing is not just to sell a product but to build a lasting relationship with your audience. This relationship, built on trust and shared values, is what transforms customers into advocates and ensures the long-term success of your brand.

CHAPTER EIGHT

# Harnessing Technology for Growth

As we transition from the digital marketing strategies discussed in the previous chapter, it is imperative to expand our lens and explore how technology can serve as a transformative force for business growth. The digital age has shifted the paradigm for how businesses operate, compete, and innovate. Technology, once a support function, has become the engine driving scalability, operational efficiency, and market dominance. In this chapter, we delve deeply into how entrepreneurs can harness technology strategically, leverage it for exponential growth, and position themselves as leaders in an increasingly tech-driven world.

The narrative of technological progress is not just about machines, algorithms, or software; it is about enabling people and businesses to achieve what was once unimaginable. Entrepreneurs, especially those at the forefront of innovation, must see technology not as a standalone asset but as an integrative force that permeates every aspect of their business.

**Operational Excellence Through Technology Integration**

In the journey of any enterprise, operational excellence serves as the cornerstone of sustainable growth. Yet achieving this requires more than just manpower - it demands systems that are agile, efficient, and data-driven. Technology acts as the catalyst to refine operations, eliminate redundancies, and unlock latent potential.

Take cloud computing as a prime example. Platforms like Amazon Web Services (AWS) and Microsoft Azure have revolutionized the way businesses store, access, and analyze data. By migrating to the cloud, companies are no longer bound by the limitations of physical infrastructure. The cloud provides unparalleled scalability, enabling a startup to function with the agility of a tech giant. For instance, Dropbox began as a simple file-sharing tool but evolved into a comprehensive cloud-based collaboration platform, empowering millions of businesses worldwide.

Automation, another pillar of operational excellence, has allowed businesses to reduce manual intervention and improve accuracy. Robotic Process Automation (RPA) tools like UiPath and Blue Prism have streamlined repetitive tasks such as data entry and invoice processing, enabling organizations to focus on strategic initiatives. The ripple effects of such innovations are profound, fostering higher employee productivity and reducing operational costs.

Customer-centric operations have also benefited immensely from technological advancements. With Customer Relationship Management (CRM) systems like Salesforce, businesses can better understand, engage with, and serve their customers. These platforms integrate data from multiple touchpoints, creating a unified view of the customer journey. This level of insight not only enhances customer satisfaction but also drives loyalty, ensuring repeat business in competitive markets.

### Transformative Power of Artificial Intelligence and Machine Learning

Artificial Intelligence (AI) and Machine Learning (ML) represent the pinnacle of technological progress, with applications that stretch across industries and functions. These technologies enable businesses to analyze vast amounts of data, make predictions, and optimize decision-making processes.

AI-driven chatbots, for example, have transformed customer service. Available 24/7, these virtual agents handle routine inquiries with remarkable efficiency, allowing human agents to focus on complex or sensitive issues. Zendesk's AI-powered customer service platform demonstrates how businesses can leverage these tools to enhance response times and improve the overall customer experience.

Beyond customer service, AI has redefined marketing, operations, and product development. By employing predictive analytics, businesses can anticipate market trends, identify customer needs, and fine-tune their offerings. Companies like Netflix have used AI to curate personalized recommendations for their users, resulting in higher engagement and customer retention rates.

Machine learning applications are equally revolutionary in industries such as healthcare, finance, and logistics. Whether it's diagnosing diseases, detecting fraud, or optimizing supply chains, ML models provide a level of precision and efficiency that was previously unattainable.

**The Internet of Things: Connecting the Physical and Digital Worlds**

The Internet of Things (IoT) has brought a new dimension to business innovation by enabling physical devices to communicate and share data. From smart homes to industrial automation, IoT applications have created new business models and improved existing processes.

Consider Nest, the smart thermostat company acquired by Google. By using IoT technology, Nest not only optimizes energy usage but also learns from user behavior to provide personalized solutions. Such innovations demonstrate how IoT can bridge the gap between user convenience and operational efficiency.

IoT's impact is particularly pronounced in industries like manufacturing and agriculture. Smart factories equipped with IoT sensors can monitor equipment performance in real time, predict maintenance needs, and minimize downtime. Similarly, IoT-enabled farming tools provide data on soil conditions, weather, and crop health, enabling farmers to make informed decisions and improve yields.

**Blockchain: A Revolution in Transparency and Security**

Blockchain technology, often associated with cryptocurrencies, has far-reaching applications that extend beyond finance. At its core, blockchain is a decentralized ledger that ensures secure, transparent, and immutable record-keeping. For businesses, this translates into opportunities to enhance trust, reduce fraud, and streamline complex processes.

Supply chain management is one area where blockchain has made significant inroads. Companies like IBM have developed blockchain solutions to track the journey of goods from source to consumer. This transparency not only improves accountability but also enables businesses to respond swiftly to disruptions, such as recalls or delays.

The intellectual property and legal sectors are also exploring blockchain's potential to protect copyrights and authenticate documents. Entrepreneurs who adopt blockchain early can differentiate themselves in markets where trust and authenticity are paramount.

**The Strategic Adoption of Emerging Technologies**

While the possibilities of technology are vast, successful integration requires strategic foresight. As Steve Jobs famously remarked, "Innovation is saying no to 1,000 things." Entrepreneurs must exercise discernment, choosing technologies that align with their business goals and deliver measurable value.

Take the case of Zoom, the video conferencing platform. Founded in 2011, Zoom identified a gap in the market for a user-friendly, reliable solution for remote communication. By prioritizing simplicity and scalability, Zoom became a lifeline for businesses and individuals during the COVID-19 pandemic. This success story underscores the importance of timing and focus in technology adoption.

5G technology is another frontier that promises to revolutionize connectivity. Its ultra-fast speeds and low latency are expected to unlock new applications in virtual reality, augmented reality, and autonomous vehicles. Entrepreneurs who prepare for the 5G era today will be well-positioned to capitalize on tomorrow's opportunities.

**Building a Tech-Driven Culture**

Implementing technology is only half the battle; fostering a culture that embraces innovation is equally critical. Employees must be equipped with the skills and mindset to adopt new tools and adapt to evolving workflows. Entrepreneurs should lead by example, championing continuous learning and collaboration across their organizations.

Moreover, cybersecurity must remain a top priority as businesses become increasingly reliant on digital systems. With data breaches and cyber threats on the rise, investing in robust security measures is not optional - it is essential for protecting customer trust and ensuring compliance with regulations.

**Conclusion**

Technology has become the great equalizer, enabling businesses of all sizes to compete on a global stage. From cloud computing and AI to IoT and blockchain, the tools for growth are more accessible than ever. However, the true measure of success lies in how these technologies are applied - not as standalone solutions but as integral parts of a larger vision.

As we turn to the next chapter, which explores the art of networking in a digitally connected world, remember that technology is a tool, not a substitute for the human element. Entrepreneurs who combine technological prowess with empathy, creativity, and strategic thinking will not only survive but thrive in the evolving landscape of global business.

CHAPTER NINE

# Effective Networking in the Modern Era

In the grand tapestry of entrepreneurship, networking has always been a vital thread. It connects ideas with opportunities, people with resources, and visionaries with the tools to realize their dreams. As we transition from the technical discussions of the previous chapters, this chapter aims to shine a light on the human side of business - networking. In our ever-evolving digital age, where algorithms dictate much of our interactions, the essence of human connection remains more relevant than ever. Networking today is a blend of traditional methods and modern digital strategies, and mastering it is not merely an asset but a necessity.

Networking is not about collecting names, business cards, or LinkedIn connections; it's about fostering genuine, lasting relationships. As Keith Ferrazzi eloquently said, "The currency of real networking is not greed but generosity." This ethos is the foundation of effective networking in both physical and virtual realms. Entrepreneurs who approach networking as a means to give rather than to take often find themselves on the receiving end of unexpected opportunities, partnerships, and growth.

**The Transformation of Networking in the Digital Era**

The digital revolution has redefined how we connect. Networking events that once revolved around physical spaces like conferences and seminars have found a counterpart in virtual spaces - LinkedIn groups, webinars, and online communities. However, the core principles of networking have not changed; they have merely adapted to new tools and platforms.

Platforms like LinkedIn have become the global hubs for professional interactions, connecting millions of users worldwide. But a presence on LinkedIn, no matter how polished, is only the beginning. To leverage its full potential, one must actively participate in the ecosystem - engaging in meaningful conversations, sharing insights, and contributing to the community.

Take, for example, the story of Sarah, a budding tech entrepreneur. When Sarah started her journey, she had little access to traditional networking circles. Instead, she turned to LinkedIn, not merely to post updates about her startup but to actively engage with her network. She commented thoughtfully on trending topics, shared her learnings through blog posts, and initiated conversations with industry leaders. Over time, this approach expanded her network beyond numbers to quality. Investors, collaborators, and even employees came into her fold because of her consistent and authentic presence. Sarah's story is a testament to how digital networking, when approached with intention and authenticity, can break barriers and create opportunities that transcend physical boundaries.

**The Power of In-Person Connections**

Despite the rise of digital tools, face-to-face networking remains irreplaceable. The nuances of human interaction - body language, tone, and eye contact - create connections that are often deeper and more memorable than their digital counterparts. Events such as conferences, trade shows, and industry meetups offer entrepreneurs unique opportunities to make lasting impressions.

Consider Marcus, a fintech entrepreneur who attended a major industry summit. Instead of spreading himself thin by trying to connect with everyone, Marcus took a focused approach. He researched the attendee list beforehand and identified individuals whose expertise aligned with his goals. During the event, Marcus engaged them in thoughtful discussions, listened actively, and demonstrated genuine interest in their work. His strategic approach not only resulted in valuable partnerships but also mentorship opportunities that significantly accelerated his company's growth.

Such interactions underscore the importance of preparation and authenticity. Networking is not a numbers game but a practice in building meaningful relationships. Even in a room full of potential connections, it's the depth of a few conversations that often yields the most rewarding outcomes.

### The Art of Building Authentic Relationships

At the heart of effective networking lies authenticity. People are naturally drawn to those who are genuine, trustworthy, and generous. This authenticity manifests in many ways - through active listening, offering help without expecting immediate returns, and being transparent about your intentions.

Active listening is perhaps the most underrated skill in networking. Many entrepreneurs fall into the trap of dominating conversations to showcase their expertise. However, true connection comes from showing interest in the other person's story, challenges, and aspirations. When you listen with intent, you not only earn trust but also uncover insights and opportunities that a surface-level interaction might miss.

### Strategic Networking Across Borders

In today's globalized world, the ability to network across cultures and time zones has become increasingly crucial. Cultural awareness is no longer optional; it's a fundamental skill for entrepreneurs looking to establish meaningful relationships in international markets. What may be considered a standard networking practice in one culture might be viewed as inappropriate or impersonal in another.

For instance, in some cultures, exchanging business cards is a ceremonial act, while in others, it's a casual gesture. Entrepreneurs who take the time to understand and respect these differences are better positioned to build trust and rapport in diverse settings. This sensitivity to cultural nuances often becomes a competitive advantage in forging global connections.

## Content Creation as Networking

In the digital age, content has become a powerful networking tool. Sharing insights through blog posts, videos, or podcasts allows entrepreneurs to establish themselves as thought leaders. This form of passive networking often attracts like-minded individuals who resonate with your perspective, creating a foundation for deeper conversations.

Jeff Bezos famously said, "Your brand is what people say about you when you're not in the room." In networking, your content is often the first impression you make. By consistently offering value through your content, you build credibility and trust within your network, even before a direct interaction takes place.

## Sustaining Relationships: The Long Game

Networking is not a one-time activity; it's a continuous process that requires effort and commitment. After meeting someone, the follow-up is critical. A personalized message referencing specific points from your conversation can leave a lasting impression. These small gestures of thoughtfulness set you apart from others and demonstrate your sincerity.

Nurturing relationships over time is equally important. Reconnecting with old contacts, expressing gratitude, and finding opportunities to collaborate or offer support are ways to keep your network alive and thriving. Networking is not just about expanding your circle; it's about deepening the connections you already have.

## Mentorship: A Networking Masterstroke

One of the most valuable outcomes of networking is the opportunity to find and become a mentor. Mentorship adds a dimension of depth to professional relationships, fostering mutual growth. For entrepreneurs, a mentor's guidance can be invaluable, providing clarity, encouragement, and access to networks that might otherwise be out of reach.

At the same time, being a mentor allows you to give back to the community, solidify your expertise, and often, gain fresh perspectives from mentees. This reciprocal relationship enriches the entrepreneurial ecosystem and strengthens your role within it.

**Conclusion**

Networking is a dynamic, evolving practice that lies at the intersection of art and science. Whether through digital platforms like LinkedIn or in-person interactions at industry events, the principles of authenticity, generosity, and strategic intent remain timeless.

As you continue your entrepreneurial journey, remember that your network is not just a list of contacts but a living, breathing ecosystem. The effort you invest in nurturing it will be repaid in ways that often surpass expectations. In the next chapter, we will delve into the realm of sales mastery and customer engagement, areas where the strength of your network will prove to be an invaluable asset. Networking, after all, is not an end in itself but a foundation upon which countless opportunities are built.

# CHAPTER TEN

# Sales Mastery and Customer Engagement

As we transition from the networking strategies discussed in the previous chapter, we now turn our attention to a critical aspect of entrepreneurship that has the power to make or break a business: sales mastery and customer engagement. The ability to close deals effectively and keep customers delighted is not just a skill - it is an art form that entrepreneurs can refine and perfect over time. This chapter delves into the intricacies of sales strategies, examines the power of empathy in handling objections, and explores inspiring stories of entrepreneurs who have built businesses with customer-centric sales approaches.

The landscape of sales has undergone a profound transformation in recent years. With the rise of digital technologies, the shift in consumer behaviors, and the growing complexity of global markets, entrepreneurs now face a web of ever-evolving customer expectations. Gone are the days of high-pressure sales tactics and generic sales pitches. Today's successful sales strategies hinge on building genuine relationships, delivering value, and understanding the unique needs of each customer.

**The New Art of Closing Deals**

When we think of sales, the traditional image that often comes to mind is that of a determined, aggressive salesperson pushing for the close. However, in the modern business world, the art of closing has undergone a transformation. It is no longer about forcing a decision or persuading someone to buy something they don't need. In today's competitive environment, effective closing is about guiding the customer on a journey - a journey of discovery where the value of your offering aligns perfectly with their needs. This approach allows the customer to arrive at the decision to purchase, not as an obligation, but as a natural progression.

One of the most powerful techniques in this new era of closing is "value-based selling." At the core of this strategy is the idea that sales should not be about pitching features or benefits. Instead, it should be about articulating the tangible value your product or service brings to the customer. For instance, if you are selling a software solution to streamline operations, you would not merely list the features of the software. Instead, you would focus on how it directly impacts the customer's operations - such as how it can save them 10 hours a week, improve team collaboration, and increase productivity by a specific percentage. By framing the conversation in terms that directly impact the customer's bottom line, you elevate your offering from a product to a solution. The conversation shifts from the question, "Why should I buy this?" to "How can I afford not to?"

Another effective closing technique, which is particularly useful in more complex sales scenarios, is the "summary close." This technique involves summarizing all the key points of agreement reached during previous discussions and reinforcing how your solution directly addresses the prospect's needs. When you recap the benefits, acknowledge the concerns that have been addressed, and highlight the value proposition, you create a narrative that naturally leads the prospect toward a final decision. The summary close works best after several rounds of negotiation or in situations where the customer has engaged in a thorough evaluation process.

However, closing is just one part of the sales equation. Equally important is the ability to handle objections with empathy and problem-solving skills. Objections are inevitable - they are a natural part of the sales process, and often, they represent a genuine concern or hesitation that the prospect may have. But they are also opportunities to further build trust, reinforce your understanding of their needs, and demonstrate the value of your offering.

**Handling Objections: The Power of Empathy and Problem-Solving**

Objections should not be seen as roadblocks, but as stepping stones to further engage with the customer and uncover deeper insights into their decision-making process. A prospect's objection is often an opportunity to address concerns, clarify misunderstandings, or provide additional information that may not have been considered previously.

The key to handling objections successfully lies in empathy. When a customer raises a concern, it's essential to approach it with curiosity rather than defensiveness. The first step is always to listen actively. Allow the customer to express their concerns fully without interruption. This approach not only shows respect but also gives you valuable information that can guide your response. Once you've fully understood the objection, it's helpful to restate the concern in your own words - this technique, known as "mirroring" - demonstrates that you are truly listening and that you care about addressing their concerns.

Validation is the next critical step. Validation does not mean agreeing with the objection, but rather acknowledging its legitimacy. For example, if a prospect objects to the price, a response such as, "I understand that budget is an important consideration. Let's take a look at how this investment could deliver value and a strong return for your business," can help reassure the prospect that you are addressing their concern in a thoughtful manner.

The next phase is problem-solving. After validating the concern, the salesperson's goal is to shift the conversation from the objection to finding a solution. This might involve offering a different perspective, providing additional data, or suggesting a tailored approach that better suits the customer's needs. The aim is not only to resolve the objection but also to deepen the relationship by demonstrating that you're not just trying to sell a product but are genuinely interested in helping the customer find the best solution.

A powerful technique for handling objections is the "feel, felt, found" method. This technique involves empathizing with how the customer feels, sharing how other clients have felt similarly, and then explaining what those clients found after they moved forward with the solution. For example, "I understand how you feel about the implementation timeline. Many of our clients initially felt the same way. However, they found that with our dedicated support team, the process was much smoother and quicker than they had anticipated."

Often, objections are not always spoken. Non-verbal cues - such as body language, tone, or even silence - can indicate underlying concerns that the customer is not voicing. Skilled entrepreneurs learn to read these subtle signals and proactively address potential objections before they become a barrier to closing the sale.

**Customer-Centric Strategies: Building Loyalty and Advocacy**

Now that we've discussed the art of closing and handling objections, it's time to focus on the broader picture: customer engagement. Closing a sale is not the end of the customer relationship; it's just the beginning. The real work starts after the transaction when the business must continue to nurture and engage the customer, ensuring their satisfaction and loyalty.

Customer engagement is about creating lasting relationships that extend beyond the transaction. It involves consistent, personalized interactions that make the customer feel valued. Many entrepreneurs make the mistake of assuming that once the sale is made, their work is done. However, the most successful companies know that the post-sale experience is just as crucial as the pre-sale process.

Take the example of Zappos, the online retail giant, which revolutionized the e-commerce world by focusing on exceptional customer service. Their customer-centric approach included offering free shipping both ways, a 365-day return policy, and a customer service department where representatives were encouraged to take as long as needed to resolve any customer issue. This commitment to customer satisfaction helped Zappos build a loyal customer base, and their focus on delighting customers resulted in explosive growth. The company grew from near-zero sales in 1999 to over $1 billion in gross sales annually by 2008. What made them stand out was not just their product offerings but their unwavering commitment to delivering an extraordinary customer experience at every touchpoint.

In the B2B world, Salesforce provides another stellar example of customer engagement. Salesforce, under the leadership of Marc Benioff, changed the way businesses thought about software. Their approach was not simply to sell a product but to forge deep partnerships with their customers. By focusing on understanding their clients' unique business challenges and offering cloud-based solutions to address them, Salesforce created a platform that was not only easy to use but also highly effective in helping clients streamline operations. Their subscription-based model, transparent pricing, and customer success programs played a pivotal role in the company's growth, positioning them as a leader in the CRM space.

Warby Parker, a direct-to-consumer eyewear company, also revolutionized the customer experience in its industry by eliminating the common pain points of buying glasses. Their home try-on program allowed customers to select five frames, try them on at home, and return them with no obligation to purchase. This unique approach not only improved the customer experience but also built trust by focusing on convenience and satisfaction, creating a loyal customer base that drove long-term success.

### The Ongoing Journey of Sales Mastery

In today's business environment, sales mastery is inextricably linked to customer engagement. Entrepreneurs who succeed are those who understand that every customer interaction is an opportunity to build a relationship, not just close a deal. They focus on delivering value, solving problems, and ensuring long-term customer satisfaction, rather than merely seeking immediate sales.

The techniques and strategies we've discussed in this chapter - such as value-based selling, empathetic objection handling, and customer-centric engagement - are not static tools but dynamic approaches that must adapt to the changing expectations of customers and the evolving market landscape. Entrepreneurs who thrive are those who stay attuned to their customers' needs, listen with empathy, and continuously seek to provide value.

As we move into the next chapter, we will explore the importance of adaptability in entrepreneurial success. We will examine how the ability to pivot with purpose and thrive in volatile markets is often the key to long-term success. The lessons learned from sales mastery and customer engagement will serve as a foundation for understanding how to adapt your business model and strategies in response to changing market dynamics and customer demands.

CHAPTER ELEVEN

# Adaptability: The Cornerstone of Growth

When you think of entrepreneurial success, you might picture innovation, hard work, or strategic thinking. While these are all crucial elements, one often-overlooked quality ties them all together: adaptability. It is the ability to anticipate change, embrace it, and evolve alongside it. This trait has become the defining characteristic of resilient entrepreneurs and organizations in an era where disruption is no longer the exception but the rule.

Adaptability is not simply a response to external pressures; it is a proactive, deliberate process of growth and transformation. It is about seeing the writing on the wall and acting before the ink dries. For entrepreneurs, adaptability is not optional - it is essential. In this chapter, we will explore how adaptability serves as the cornerstone of sustainable growth, drawing on compelling stories, real-world examples, and actionable insights that illuminate its power.

**The Nature of Adaptability**

Adaptability is not about losing oneself in a sea of trends or abandoning core values at the first sign of trouble. Instead, it's a balance between flexibility and steadfastness. It requires a clear vision, yet an openness to altering the path toward achieving it. Adaptability means knowing when to stay the course and when to pivot.

Let's draw a distinction:

1. **Reactive Adaptability**: This involves responding to change after it occurs. For example, a company might adjust its marketing strategy in response to declining sales.
2. **Proactive Adaptability**: This is foresight-driven. It involves anticipating change and positioning oneself ahead of the curve. Think of businesses that began investing in AI and machine learning years before these technologies became mainstream.

Proactive adaptability is the mark of visionary entrepreneurs. It demonstrates not just the capacity to respond but the wisdom to foresee.

### Why Adaptability is the Cornerstone of Growth

Adaptability underpins every aspect of entrepreneurship. Markets are inherently volatile; customers' needs evolve, competitors emerge, and global disruptions like pandemics or technological revolutions rewrite the rules of the game. Entrepreneurs who fail to adapt risk becoming obsolete.

**Navigating Uncertainty**: Adaptable entrepreneurs thrive amid ambiguity. They understand that uncertainty is not something to be feared but a fertile ground for innovation.

**Seizing Opportunities**: Change often brings new opportunities. Those who adapt quickly can capitalize on shifts before their competitors.

**Building Resilience**: Businesses with adaptability baked into their culture are better equipped to weather storms and come out stronger.

### Lessons from Entrepreneurial Giants

To truly grasp the transformative power of adaptability, let's delve into some stories of businesses that have either mastered or failed to master this trait.

**The Netflix Revolution**

Netflix's journey from a DVD rental service to a global streaming giant is the quintessential example of adaptability. In the late 2000s, as streaming technology became viable, Netflix executives saw the potential for a massive industry shift. While their DVD rental business was still profitable, they began to transition toward streaming.

The decision wasn't easy. It required heavy investments in technology, acquiring content licenses, and educating a market that was just beginning to understand streaming. Critics questioned the move, but Netflix's adaptability paid off. Today, it dominates the entertainment industry, leaving less adaptive competitors like Blockbuster in the dust.

**Kodak's Cautionary Tale**

In contrast, Kodak's failure to adapt offers a sobering lesson. Despite inventing the first digital camera in 1975, Kodak hesitated to embrace the technology for fear of cannibalizing its lucrative film business. By the time Kodak finally acted, digital photography had become the norm, and competitors had seized the market. Kodak's reluctance to adapt led to its downfall, proving that even giants can crumble when they resist change.

**Pivoting with Purpose**

Adaptability often requires pivoting - a deliberate shift in business strategy to align with changing circumstances. However, not all pivots are created equal. The most successful ones are grounded in a clear understanding of the company's strengths and market dynamics.

**Airbnb: A Pandemic Pivot**

When the COVID-19 pandemic brought global travel to a halt, Airbnb's core business was under threat. Instead of waiting for the situation to improve, the company adapted swiftly. They launched the "Go Near" campaign, promoting local stays and experiences. Additionally, Airbnb enhanced its cleaning protocols to reassure customers about safety.

This pivot not only helped Airbnb weather the crisis but also expanded its appeal to new customer segments. It's a testament to the power of purpose-driven adaptability - aligning short-term actions with long-term vision.

### Building a Culture of Adaptability

For entrepreneurs, personal adaptability is only part of the equation. True success requires creating an organizational culture where adaptability thrives.

### Fostering an Adaptive Workforce

**Encourage Experimentation**: Allow employees to test new ideas without fear of failure. Failures, when viewed as learning experiences, often lead to breakthroughs.

**Promote Cross-Functional Collaboration**: Teams that work across silos can generate more creative solutions to complex problems.

**Invest in Continuous Learning**: Provide opportunities for employees to upskill and stay abreast of industry trends.

Google's "20% time" policy, which encourages employees to spend a portion of their time on passion projects, is a shining example of fostering adaptability. Many of Google's most successful innovations, including Gmail and Google Maps, originated from this policy.

### Adaptability in Leadership

Entrepreneurs must lead by example. Jeff Bezos' "Day 1" philosophy at Amazon captures this perfectly. By treating every day as if it were the first day of the company, Bezos ensured that Amazon remained innovative, customer-focused, and ready to adapt.

### Adaptability in Practice: A Framework

Adaptability can feel abstract, but it's a skill that can be cultivated. Here's a practical framework to incorporate adaptability into your entrepreneurial journey:

**Scan the Horizon**: Regularly monitor market trends, customer feedback, and competitor activities.

**Be Data-Driven**: Use analytics to identify early signs of change and assess the effectiveness of adaptations.

**Start Small**: Test changes on a smaller scale before rolling them out company-wide.

**Celebrate Agility**: Recognize and reward adaptability within your team to reinforce its importance.

## Case Studies: Adaptability in Action

### Domino's: From Pizza to Tech

Domino's Pizza once struggled with poor brand perception and stagnant sales. Recognizing the rising importance of technology in consumer behavior, Domino's reinvented itself as a tech-driven company. Innovations like the pizza tracker, voice-ordering capabilities, and even experimenting with delivery drones have made Domino's a leader in customer experience.

### Fujifilm's Reinvention

When digital cameras disrupted the film market, Fujifilm diversified into healthcare, cosmetics, and other industries by leveraging its expertise in chemicals and imaging technology. This bold move saved the company and enabled it to thrive in entirely new markets.

### The Entrepreneurial Mindset of Adaptability

Adaptability starts within. Entrepreneurs must cultivate a mindset that embraces change, views failure as a stepping stone, and remains curious about the unknown. This involves:

- **Resilience**: The ability to recover quickly from setbacks.
- **Curiosity**: A desire to explore emerging trends and technologies.
- **Self-Awareness**: Understanding your strengths, weaknesses, and when to seek help.

**Conclusion: Adaptability as a Lifelong Companion**

Adaptability is not a one-time effort; it is a lifelong practice. As entrepreneurs, the journey will always be marked by uncertainty. Embracing adaptability ensures that you not only survive but thrive in this ever-changing landscape.

The companies that endure are not necessarily the strongest or the most innovative - they are the ones that adapt. As we prepare to explore the importance of building and leading dynamic teams in the next chapter, remember that adaptability is the glue that holds every entrepreneurial effort together. It is the cornerstone of growth and the ultimate differentiator in a competitive world.

CHAPTER TWELVE

# Building and Leading Teams

Building and leading a team is one of the most profound and enduring challenges of entrepreneurship. A company is not just the sum of its products, services, or strategies - it is the people who bring those elements to life. Behind every great business stands a cohesive team, united by a shared vision and driven by a collective sense of purpose. The art of assembling such a team, nurturing its potential, and steering it toward success lies at the heart of effective leadership.

In this chapter, we delve into the essential components of team building: creating a vibrant and innovative company culture, empowering and engaging employees, and learning from the stories of companies that have set the gold standard in workplace excellence. To build a team that thrives, you must not only recognize the importance of these elements but also commit to weaving them into the fabric of your leadership philosophy.

**The Foundation of Team Success**

Every successful team begins with clarity - a shared vision that defines the organization's purpose and a set of values that guide its actions. Vision acts as a lighthouse, offering direction during calm seas and turbulent storms. It is not enough to articulate a lofty goal; leaders must embed this vision into every aspect of the team's operation, ensuring that each individual understands their role in the broader mission.

Values, on the other hand, provide the moral compass. They create a framework for decision-making, shape interactions within the team, and foster a sense of unity. Consider the example of Patagonia, the outdoor apparel company. Their unwavering commitment to environmental sustainability has not only informed their business strategies but also attracted a workforce deeply aligned with their mission. This alignment has proven to be a powerful driver of innovation and loyalty, both internally and among customers.

As an entrepreneur, the task of building a team goes beyond recruitment. It involves creating an environment where people feel connected to the mission and empowered to contribute their best.

**Creating a Culture of Innovation**

Culture is the soul of an organization. It determines how employees interact, approach challenges, and perceive their work. A culture that fosters innovation does not arise spontaneously; it is cultivated through deliberate actions and thoughtful leadership.

One of the cornerstones of an innovative culture is psychological safety. When team members feel safe to express ideas, question norms, and take calculated risks without fear of judgment, creativity flourishes. This concept gained widespread attention through Google's "Project Aristotle," a study that identified psychological safety as the most critical factor in team performance.

Creating such an environment requires leaders to model vulnerability, encourage open dialogue, and celebrate both successes and failures as learning opportunities. It is in this climate of trust that breakthroughs are born.

Curiosity, too, is essential. Leaders must actively nurture curiosity by encouraging their teams to explore new ideas and challenge conventional wisdom. Netflix provides an illustrative example. Early in its history, Netflix recognized the limitations of its DVD rental business model and pivoted boldly to streaming content - a move that transformed the entertainment industry. This willingness to question and adapt stemmed from a culture that valued innovation above comfort.

Rewarding experimentation further reinforces an innovative culture. Mistakes, rather than being punished, should be viewed as stepping stones to success. Leaders who acknowledge the effort behind bold attempts - regardless of the outcome - create a sense of psychological freedom that fuels ingenuity.

Lastly, diversity and inclusion play a critical role. A diverse team brings varied perspectives, fostering richer discussions and more comprehensive solutions. It is through these differences that organizations discover their competitive edge.

**Empowering and Engaging Employees**

An empowered employee is an engaged employee, and engaged employees form the backbone of any thriving organization. Empowerment begins with trust. Leaders must trust their teams to make decisions, solve problems, and take ownership of their work. In turn, employees who feel trusted are more likely to rise to the occasion, demonstrating initiative and accountability.

Clear communication is vital in building this trust. Employees must understand their roles, the organization's goals, and how their contributions fit into the bigger picture. Without this clarity, even the most talented individuals can feel lost or undervalued.

Beyond clarity, opportunities for growth are essential. Leaders who invest in the development of their employees - whether through training, mentorship, or career advancement programs - signal that they value their team members not just as workers but as individuals. This sense of personal investment fosters loyalty and motivation.

Recognition is another powerful tool for engagement. A simple acknowledgment of effort or achievement can have a profound impact on morale. Whether through formal awards or informal expressions of gratitude, recognizing the contributions of your team reinforces their value and inspires continued excellence.

Consider the story of Zappos, the online shoe retailer. Renowned for its exceptional workplace culture, Zappos has built an environment where employees feel valued and engaged. From their focus on personal development to their quirky office traditions, Zappos has demonstrated that happy employees are the foundation of happy customers - a philosophy that has become their competitive advantage.

**Leadership: The Art of Inspiration**

At the heart of every successful team is a leader who inspires trust and provides direction. Leadership is not merely about issuing commands; it is about guiding the team with empathy, vision, and authenticity. Great leaders understand that their role is to serve their team, removing obstacles, providing resources, and fostering an environment where individuals can thrive.

Empathy is one of the most important qualities of effective leadership. By understanding the needs, aspirations, and challenges of their team members, leaders can build stronger relationships and create a supportive atmosphere. Vision, too, is critical. A leader must not only articulate a compelling goal but also inspire their team to believe in it and work towards it with passion.

Authenticity, meanwhile, builds trust. A leader who is genuine, transparent, and consistent earns the respect and loyalty of their team. This authenticity becomes the bedrock of a resilient, high-performing team.

**The Challenges of Team Building**

Building and leading a team is not without its challenges. Conflict, misalignment, and varying levels of motivation are inevitable. However, proactive leadership can transform these challenges into opportunities for growth.

For instance, conflicts, when managed effectively, can lead to greater understanding and stronger relationships. Addressing issues openly and constructively ensures that disagreements do not fester but instead contribute to the team's evolution.

Maintaining motivation, particularly in the face of setbacks, requires leaders to be attuned to the needs of their team. Regular check-ins, celebrating milestones, and fostering a positive environment are critical to sustaining morale.

Finally, aligning diverse perspectives can be a challenge, but it is also one of the greatest strengths of a well-constructed team. Leaders who facilitate open dialogue and encourage collaboration harness the power of diversity to achieve exceptional results.

**Lessons from Workplace Excellence**

The stories of companies like Netflix, Zappos, and Patagonia illustrate that building and leading a team is both a science and an art. These organizations have demonstrated that a strong culture, empowered employees, and inspired leadership are the hallmarks of enduring success.

As an entrepreneur, the legacy you leave will be shaped not only by the products you create or the profits you generate but by the people you lead. Your team is a reflection of your vision, values, and leadership. Invest in them, inspire them, and empower them to build something extraordinary.

In the next chapter, we will explore the role of strategic partnerships in scaling a business. But remember, no partnership can replace the value of a strong, united team working towards a common goal. They are, and will always be, the heart of your entrepreneurial journey.

CHAPTER THIRTEEN

# Leadership Essentials for Entrepreneurs

Leadership is the linchpin of any successful entrepreneurial journey. While the founder's vision sets the initial trajectory, it is effective leadership that ensures sustainability, growth, and transformation. Leadership in the entrepreneurial world is multifaceted - it demands emotional intelligence, a willingness to adapt, and the ability to inspire teams through challenges and triumphs. This chapter delves deeply into the nuances of leadership, exploring how emotional intelligence shapes decision-making, the critical transition from founder to leader, and invaluable lessons drawn from the experiences of industry pioneers.

## The Emotional Core of Leadership

At its essence, leadership is about relationships. It is the ability to connect with people on a level that inspires trust, commitment, and collaboration. This human-centric approach is powered by emotional intelligence (EI), a concept popularized by Daniel Goleman. EI is not just a buzzword; it is a measurable and actionable framework that separates exceptional leaders from the rest.

Emotional intelligence begins with **self-awareness** - an honest appraisal of one's own emotions, biases, and behavioural patterns. Entrepreneurs are often engrossed in their vision, but without self-awareness, they risk alienating their teams or making impulsive decisions. For instance, when Howard Schultz returned to Starbucks during a period of stagnation, his ability to reflect on past missteps allowed him to realign the company with its core values of customer experience and innovation.

Self-awareness is complemented by **self-regulation**, the capacity to manage one's emotions, especially under pressure. Entrepreneurs frequently face high-stakes situations, from securing investments to managing crises. A leader who remains composed during turmoil not only makes better decisions but also instills confidence in their team. Think of Nelson Mandela, who exemplified self-regulation by maintaining his composure and optimism during 27 years of imprisonment - a quality that later empowered him to lead a divided South Africa.

**Empathy**, another pillar of EI, is the bridge that connects leaders to their teams, customers, and stakeholders. Empathetic leaders prioritize understanding over judgment, actively listening to concerns and perspectives. Indra Nooyi, former CEO of PepsiCo, demonstrated empathy through her practice of acknowledging employees' personal sacrifices. This small but powerful gesture humanized her leadership and fostered a culture of mutual respect.

**Social skills**, the outward manifestation of emotional intelligence, are equally vital. These skills encompass clear communication, conflict resolution, and the ability to build lasting relationships. Leaders with strong social skills are natural collaborators, mediators, and motivators. Whether it's Elon Musk rallying his engineers at SpaceX or Oprah Winfrey connecting with millions through authenticity, social skills are the glue that holds effective leadership together.

Finally, **motivation** drives leaders to persist despite setbacks and challenges. Unlike external rewards, this motivation stems from an intrinsic belief in the purpose of their work. Steve Jobs epitomized this when he returned to Apple in 1997. His relentless pursuit of perfection and innovation led to the creation of iconic products like the iPhone, which redefined entire industries.

### From Founder to Leader: A Transformational Shift

Founders often launch their ventures with a singular focus: survival. The early days are a whirlwind of multitasking, where the founder is not only the visionary but also the marketer, accountant, and product manager. However, as a company scales, this hands-on approach becomes unsustainable. Transitioning from a founder to a leader is both a necessity and a challenge.

One of the first steps in this transition is mastering the art of **delegation**. Entrepreneurs frequently grapple with the notion that "no one can do it better than me." While this mindset may serve them in the early stages, it becomes a bottleneck as the organization grows. Effective leaders trust their teams to take ownership, empowering them with autonomy and accountability. For instance, Jeff Bezos famously focused on building a leadership team that could make independent, high-stakes decisions, freeing him to concentrate on Amazon's long-term strategy.

Another critical aspect is developing **strategic foresight**. Founders are often preoccupied with immediate concerns - launching products, acquiring customers, and managing cash flow. Leaders, however, think in terms of the company's five-, ten-, or even twenty-year future. This requires balancing short-term wins with long-term investments.

Transitioning to leadership also demands **letting go of ego**. Founders may find it challenging to relinquish control or accept feedback, but true leaders view constructive criticism as a growth opportunity. Jack Ma, co-founder of Alibaba, frequently emphasized learning from failures and surrounding himself with individuals smarter than him. This humility allowed him to guide Alibaba from an online marketplace to a global e-commerce giant.

Finally, leaders must learn to **scale culture**. In the early days, culture is often an extension of the founder's personality. As the team grows, preserving and evolving that culture becomes a deliberate act. Airbnb's Brian Chesky focused on embedding the company's core values into every aspect of operations, ensuring that even as the organization scaled globally, its commitment to "belonging" remained intact.

### Wisdom from the Titans of Industry

The entrepreneurial landscape is rich with examples of leaders whose philosophies and practices have left indelible marks on their industries. These stories provide both inspiration and practical lessons for aspiring leaders.

**1. Elon Musk: Innovating Beyond Limits**
Elon Musk's leadership is defined by his ability to inspire audacious thinking. Whether it's revolutionizing transportation with Tesla or aiming to colonize Mars with SpaceX, Musk's relentless focus on innovation challenges conventional boundaries. His journey underscores the importance of aligning leadership with purpose - when the leader's vision is clear, teams are willing to push the limits of possibility.

**2. Sheryl Sandberg: Leading with Empathy and Action**
As COO of Facebook, Sheryl Sandberg brought a unique blend of strategic thinking and emotional intelligence to the company. Her advocacy for gender equality in the workplace, exemplified by her book *Lean In*, demonstrates that leadership extends beyond corporate goals to encompass societal impact. Sandberg's approach reminds us that leaders are role models who shape not only organizations but also the world around them.

**3. Ratan Tata: Leading with Integrity**
Ratan Tata, the visionary leader behind the Tata Group, is celebrated for his ethical leadership. Under his guidance, the company expanded globally while maintaining its commitment to social responsibility. Tata's focus on integrity, humility, and employee welfare highlights the role of values in long-term success.

### Leadership: A Lifelong Endeavor

Leadership is not a skill that can be mastered overnight; it is a lifelong journey of growth, learning, and adaptation. The entrepreneurial path is fraught with challenges, but each obstacle presents an opportunity to refine leadership capabilities.

The most enduring leaders are those who blend vision with empathy, decisiveness with humility, and strategy with adaptability. They understand that leadership is not about commanding from the front but about empowering others to reach their fullest potential.

As we move forward, the next chapter will explore the art of building strategic partnerships - an extension of leadership that multiplies opportunities and drives collaborative success. However, remember that even the most powerful alliances rest on the foundation of trust and vision cultivated by effective leadership. Leadership is not merely about guiding others; it is about inspiring them to embark on a journey of shared discovery and achievement.

In this evolving narrative of leadership, it is imperative to understand that the most remarkable leaders are not those who simply dictate the terms of engagement but those who create an environment where ideas flourish, challenges are embraced, and every individual feels intrinsically tied to the organization's purpose.

Great leaders don't just adapt to the world around them; they shape it. They anticipate changes and position their teams to thrive within new paradigms. The ability to lead effectively is rooted in a commitment to personal growth and a willingness to continuously refine one's leadership style in response to new insights and experiences.

**The Legacy of Leadership**

Leadership is as much about the legacy you leave behind as it is about the day-to-day decisions you make. A leader's impact is measured not only by the success of their organization but by the leaders they nurture along the way.

Think of how Steve Jobs mentored Tim Cook, ensuring Apple's seamless transition and continued growth. Similarly, Mary Barra, the CEO of General Motors, climbed the ranks under the mentorship of leaders who believed in empowering future talent. These examples demonstrate that leadership is inherently generative - it's about creating a cycle of inspiration and empowerment that outlasts your tenure.

To leave a lasting legacy, leaders must focus on cultivating resilience within their teams. This means teaching them how to navigate uncertainty, encouraging innovative problem-solving, and fostering a mindset of continuous learning. Organizations that prioritize these qualities in their leaders often find themselves better prepared to weather challenges and capitalize on opportunities.

Moreover, the legacy of a leader is also enshrined in the culture they build. Company culture isn't just a buzzword - it's the lifeblood of any organization. It is the set of shared values, beliefs, and behaviors that guide how work gets done. A strong culture can inspire teams to give their best, attract top talent, and create an identity that customers trust and respect. Leaders who understand this and invest in their organizational culture are setting their companies up for long-term success.

**Looking Ahead**

As we close this chapter on leadership essentials, remember that leadership is not a destination but a continuous journey. It is shaped by your ability to learn, your willingness to listen, and your determination to grow. The entrepreneurial world is dynamic, and leaders must be dynamic too, evolving alongside their businesses and the people they serve.

In the next chapter, we will delve into the intricate art of building strategic partnerships and alliances. These relationships are often the catalysts for exponential growth, opening doors to resources, expertise, and markets that might otherwise remain out of reach. Leadership plays a pivotal role in forging these connections, ensuring that partnerships are not just transactional but transformative.

Leadership is the heartbeat of entrepreneurship. It sets the rhythm for innovation, collaboration, and resilience. And as you embark on your journey as a leader, let this chapter serve as both a roadmap and a source of inspiration, reminding you that every decision you make has the power to shape not just the future of your organization, but the lives of those who follow your lead.

With these lessons in mind, let us continue to explore the broader world of entrepreneurship, where leadership, vision, and strategy converge to create lasting impact.

CHAPTER FOURTEEN

# Productivity and Time Management

The life of an entrepreneur is a delicate balance between vision and execution, creativity and practicality. But more than anything else, it's about managing the most precious resource of all: time. The challenges of entrepreneurship are vast, with long hours, seemingly endless to-do lists, and constant pressure to achieve ambitious goals. With so much to juggle, how do successful entrepreneurs stay on top of their responsibilities without sacrificing their personal lives or burning out? The answer lies in mastering the art of productivity and time management - skills that are vital to scaling a business, leading a team, and maintaining personal well-being.

In this chapter, we will explore the tactics, tools, and mindset required to optimize time and productivity. We'll delve into practical strategies for entrepreneurs facing high-stress environments and offer insights on how to handle mounting workloads while maintaining focus. Through the stories of entrepreneurs who've overcome time constraints, we'll uncover lessons that you can apply in your own journey.

**The Science of Focus: How to Maximize Your Productivity**

In the entrepreneurial world, distractions are relentless. Your phone rings, your inbox fills up, meetings pile on, and urgent tasks keep surfacing. It's easy to feel as though you're always playing catch-up, struggling to keep everything afloat. But what separates the most successful entrepreneurs from the rest is their ability to block out these distractions and stay focused on what truly matters.

One of the most effective ways to improve focus is by structuring your environment to minimize distractions. This might sound simple, but it's a strategy that many entrepreneurs overlook. If your workspace is cluttered or filled with constant noise and interruptions, your ability to focus will be severely hindered. Elon Musk, known for his hyper-focus, emphasizes the importance of deep, uninterrupted work. He famously schedules time in his calendar for "no meetings" blocks, ensuring that he can immerse himself fully in high-priority tasks without distractions.

Another important tactic for improving focus is to prioritize your tasks based on their impact. Entrepreneurs often feel compelled to handle a multitude of tasks each day, but not all tasks are created equal. Some may seem urgent but have little long-term value, while others may be less time-sensitive but critical to the success of the business. A key strategy here is the **Eisenhower Matrix**, which helps entrepreneurs distinguish between urgent and important tasks. By using this matrix, you can categorize your daily activities into four quadrants:

**Urgent and important:** Tasks that require immediate attention and align with your long-term goals.

**Important but not urgent:** Tasks that are crucial for business growth but don't need immediate attention.

**Urgent but not important:** Tasks that require quick action but don't contribute significantly to your objectives.

**Neither urgent nor important:** Low-value tasks that should be minimized or delegated.

By identifying and focusing on the most important tasks, you can avoid the trap of spending your days responding to "urgent" matters that don't truly move your business forward.

While focus is essential, so is mental and physical well-being. A well-rested mind and body are far more productive than one bogged down by fatigue. The human brain has limitations in terms of how much it can concentrate effectively. Studies show that after about 90 minutes of focused work, cognitive performance begins to decline. For this reason, many successful entrepreneurs swear by the Pomodoro Technique, a time management system that alternates between 25-minute intervals of focused work and 5-minute breaks. These breaks are designed to recharge the brain, allowing you to maintain high levels of productivity throughout the day.

**Managing Growing Teams: The Challenge of Scaling Operations**

As your business expands, so does the complexity of managing your time. In the early days of entrepreneurship, you wear many hats - chief marketer, financial officer, product designer, and more. But as your company grows, it becomes increasingly difficult to maintain control over all aspects of the operation. This is when your time management strategy must evolve.

Delegation becomes one of the most important skills to develop as your team expands. The best entrepreneurs recognize that they can't do everything themselves, and empowering others is essential for sustainable growth. However, successful delegation requires more than just handing off tasks - it requires trust and clear communication. You must ensure that your team has the resources, skills, and autonomy to complete their tasks effectively. This is where project management tools like Asana, Trello, and Basecamp can be incredibly helpful. These tools allow you to track progress on tasks, communicate efficiently with your team, and ensure that nothing falls through the cracks.

But delegation isn't just about giving tasks to others; it's about aligning those tasks with the overall vision and goals of the business. By setting clear expectations and breaking down larger projects into manageable pieces, you allow your team to take ownership and contribute meaningfully to the success of the company.

Take the case of **Zappos**, the online shoe retailer. In its early days, CEO Tony Hsieh spent a lot of time directly overseeing operations. But as the company grew, Hsieh had to shift his focus towards leadership and culture. One of the key strategies he implemented was to give his employees the freedom to make decisions on behalf of the company. He empowered them to act in the best interests of customers, even if it meant going outside the established processes. This approach of decentralized decision-making helped Zappos scale rapidly while maintaining a high level of customer satisfaction and engagement.

Another aspect of managing time as you scale your business is ensuring that you don't lose sight of your core mission and values. In times of rapid growth, it's easy to become bogged down by operational minutiae and lose sight of the big picture. This is why many entrepreneurs emphasize the importance of **company culture** - a shared sense of purpose that keeps everyone on the same page. A strong culture helps maintain alignment across the organization and allows employees to make decisions that support the company's long-term vision, even in your absence.

## Mastering Time Constraints: Stories of Entrepreneurs Who Overcame the Odds

Time constraints are a reality that every entrepreneur must face. Whether you're dealing with a tight deadline, limited resources, or unexpected obstacles, the ability to adapt and make the most of limited time is what sets successful entrepreneurs apart.

Consider the story of **Sara Blakely**, the founder of Spanx. Blakely started her business with only $5,000 and worked out of a spare bedroom, often juggling her responsibilities as a salesperson at the same time. She didn't have the luxury of spending all day in a corporate office, but she made time to refine her product and develop her brand. Blakely's commitment to time management and her ability to prioritize the most crucial aspects of her business allowed her to build Spanx into a billion-dollar empire.

Another example comes from **Richard Branson**, the founder of Virgin Group. Branson is a master of multitasking, but he also knows the importance of taking time for himself. He emphasizes the need for entrepreneurs to manage their time wisely and create a work-life balance that allows them to recharge. For Branson, this means spending time with his family, playing sports, and finding moments of adventure outside of work. By prioritizing his personal life, Branson ensures that he has the energy and creativity to focus on his business endeavours.

Even when time is not on their side, entrepreneurs like **Howard Schultz** (CEO of Starbucks) and **Reed Hastings** (CEO of Netflix) have shown remarkable ability to make bold, time-sensitive decisions that led to their companies' success. In the case of Schultz, the decision to offer healthcare benefits to part-time employees in 1988 was a bold one, driven by a belief in the value of investing in employees - even during the company's early, challenging years. Similarly, Reed Hastings' decision to pivot Netflix from a DVD rental service to a streaming platform in the early 2000s was driven by foresight and a recognition of changing market dynamics.

**Conclusion: Time as the Ultimate Lever for Success**

In the end, time is the greatest asset of an entrepreneur. While you cannot control the number of hours in a day, you can control how you use that time. Entrepreneurs who master time management are those who recognize that productivity isn't about doing more things - it's about doing the right things, with focus and intention.

By cultivating discipline, utilizing tools that streamline operations, and developing a mindset that prioritizes what truly matters, you can ensure that your time is spent building the future you envision.

As we conclude this chapter, it's essential to recognize that effective time management is not a static skill but an evolving one. As your business grows, your time management strategies will need to adapt as well. But the principles of focus, delegation, and intentionality will always remain crucial to your success. In the following chapter, we will delve into how financial management plays a critical role in the entrepreneurial journey, another area where time - and your ability to control it - can determine your business's trajectory.

CHAPTER FIFTEEN

# Managing Risk and Planning for Crises

Entrepreneurship is a journey laden with unexpected challenges and opportunities. The path is rarely straight, and the road ahead is often unclear, as entrepreneurs encounter uncharted territories, shifting market demands, and evolving technologies. One of the most formidable tasks any entrepreneur faces is managing risk while planning for inevitable crises. Business risks are not only financial - they span operational, strategic, technological, and even reputational threats. With an ever-changing landscape, the ability to anticipate, assess, and mitigate these risks is what distinguishes successful businesses from those that falter under pressure.

## The Importance of Proactive Risk Management

While some risks are inevitable, the most successful entrepreneurs take a proactive approach to managing them. Proactive risk management is about identifying potential threats before they escalate and preparing a response that minimizes harm. It involves both the mindset and the strategic implementation of processes that help mitigate risk exposure. By understanding that risk is a constant in business, entrepreneurs can ensure that they are prepared, not only to react when things go wrong, but to prevent those risks from affecting their long-term success.

One of the first steps in proactive risk management is the identification of key risks. Entrepreneurs must adopt a comprehensive perspective, considering various facets of their business. This includes financial risks, operational risks, legal risks, and even external threats like changes in the regulatory landscape or shifts in customer behavior.

**SWOT Analysis** - an assessment tool evaluating a business's Strengths, Weaknesses, Opportunities, and Threats - is an excellent starting point. By objectively examining internal strengths and weaknesses alongside external opportunities and threats, entrepreneurs gain a clearer picture of where vulnerabilities lie. Identifying threats within the context of industry shifts, competitor actions, or market volatility can help prepare the business for any challenges that might arise.

Financial forecasting is another pillar of risk management. Entrepreneurs must remain vigilant about their cash flow and maintain realistic projections about revenues, expenditures, and profitability. This forecasting helps to identify periods of financial strain, potential cash shortages, or overextension. Techniques like **sensitivity analysis** allow businesses to model different financial outcomes based on variables like changing market conditions or unexpected costs. Armed with this information, entrepreneurs can make better decisions, from scaling operations to curbing spending in lean periods.

One key concept that often gets overlooked in risk management is **diversification**. When businesses become overly reliant on a single customer, supplier, or product, they expose themselves to severe risks if any of these factors are disrupted. Diversifying revenue streams and suppliers, and even exploring new markets, is one of the most effective ways to shield the business from external shocks. By broadening the company's focus, entrepreneurs create a buffer against volatility in any one area.

As businesses grow, the complexity of their risk management needs also evolves. Large organizations require structured **risk management frameworks**, often involving a dedicated team or even an entire department that continually assesses risks across various business functions. This team is responsible for implementing risk mitigation strategies, ensuring compliance, and keeping leadership informed about potential threats.

**Crisis Management: Planning for the Worst-Case Scenario**

No matter how meticulously you plan or how careful you are in identifying risks, the reality is that crises will happen. Whether it's a global economic downturn, a natural disaster, a cybersecurity breach, or a sudden loss of a key business partner, crises can throw any business off course. The key to navigating these moments is **preparedness**. Just as you plan for business growth, you must also plan for business decline, recognizing that crisis situations require rapid decision-making, clear communication, and an unwavering focus on survival.

Effective crisis management begins long before the crisis strikes. Building a **crisis management plan** ensures that your business is not caught off guard when disaster strikes. The plan should define exactly what constitutes a crisis for your organization, outline the specific steps that will be taken in response, and assign roles and responsibilities to key team members. A clear crisis plan allows leadership to act swiftly and confidently, without having to spend valuable time trying to figure out what to do in the moment.

A critical component of this plan is **communication**. In times of crisis, the way you communicate can make or break your business. Clear, honest, and timely communication with employees, customers, investors, and other stakeholders is essential for maintaining trust and minimizing damage to your brand's reputation. **Internal communication protocols** must be established to ensure that employees are kept in the loop regarding the situation and what steps the organization is taking. Similarly, **external communication** - whether through press releases, social media, or direct customer communication - must be handled with transparency and empathy.

One of the most important aspects of crisis management is **leadership**. During a crisis, people look to leaders for direction, reassurance, and stability. It is in these moments that the true strength of leadership is tested. A leader must remain calm, show decisiveness, and demonstrate a willingness to make difficult decisions.

Take the example of **Johnson & Johnson** during the 1982 Tylenol crisis. When seven people died after ingesting Tylenol capsules that had been tampered with, the company faced an unimaginable crisis. The leadership team immediately made the decision to recall 31 million bottles of Tylenol, even though it would cost them millions of dollars. They also initiated a public safety campaign to regain consumer trust. Their commitment to consumer safety, coupled with transparent communication, helped Johnson & Johnson recover its reputation and emerge as a stronger company. This example demonstrates the importance of **taking immediate action, prioritizing customer safety, and restoring trust** during a crisis.

**Business continuity planning** is another crucial element of crisis preparation. No matter how severe the disruption, a continuity plan ensures that essential operations can continue or be quickly restored. It outlines which functions are critical to the business's survival, and how those functions can be maintained during times of crisis. For instance, can your team work remotely in the event of a natural disaster? Do you have backup suppliers or service providers in place in case of disruption? Business continuity planning also extends to technology, ensuring that critical data is backed up and that cybersecurity measures are in place to protect against cyberattacks.

**Examples of Resilience: Surviving Economic Downturns**

Economic downturns are some of the most common types of crises that businesses must face. Whether it's a global recession, financial crisis, or industry-specific downturn, these events can severely impact a company's bottom line. However, history shows that some businesses not only survive economic downturns but emerge from them stronger and more competitive.

**Netflix** is one of the most remarkable examples of a company that survived and thrived during economic downturns. When the global financial crisis hit in 2008, many companies in the entertainment industry saw a decline in demand. Yet, Netflix managed to grow by focusing on its subscription-based model and shifting its focus to streaming services. At a time when people were cutting back on discretionary spending, Netflix offered an affordable alternative to traditional cable television. This strategic pivot allowed Netflix to increase its user base and emerge from the crisis with a stronger market position.

Similarly, **Apple** survived the 1997 dot-com bubble burst, which saw many tech companies crash under the weight of overvaluation. At the time, Apple was on the brink of bankruptcy, and many questioned its long-term viability. However, the company's leadership, under Steve Jobs, made bold moves to streamline product lines and refocus on innovation. Jobs's vision and Apple's subsequent product releases, such as the iPod and iPhone, revolutionized the tech industry, ensuring Apple's place as a leader in consumer electronics.

During the **2008 financial crisis**, companies like **General Electric (GE)** and **Ford** faced significant pressure but managed to weather the storm through tough decisions and strong leadership. GE's then-CEO, Jeff Immelt, focused on restructuring the company and prioritizing its most profitable divisions. Ford, on the other hand, avoided government bailouts by taking proactive measures to reduce debt, restructure operations, and focus on innovation. These companies serve as examples of how strong leadership and decisive action can guide a business through even the toughest economic conditions.

## Turning Risk Into Opportunity

While risk and crisis are inevitable, the way we approach them makes all the difference. The most successful entrepreneurs are those who view risk not as a threat, but as an opportunity to innovate, diversify, and grow. Risk is not something to be feared; it is an essential part of business evolution. In every crisis lies the potential for transformation, and in every risk lies the potential for reward.

The future is uncertain, but the entrepreneurs who navigate that uncertainty with foresight, resilience, and agility will always find a way to not just survive, but thrive. By developing strong risk management practices, creating effective crisis plans, and learning from past challenges, entrepreneurs can build businesses that are not only capable of withstanding crises but are also positioned to capitalize on the opportunities that follow.

As we move forward into the next chapter, we'll explore how mastering **financial management** in uncertain times can help sustain and propel your business toward greater success. Financial stewardship, after all, is the foundation that supports all business strategies, and in times of crisis, it becomes your most powerful tool for survival and growth.

## CHAPTER SIXTEEN

# Continuous Feedback for Innovation

Innovation is often romanticized as a flash of genius, a eureka moment that changes the course of history. But in real,ity, it's rarely a solo endeavour. Behind every groundbreaking idea or product lies an iterative process powered by feedback - a cycle of listening, adapting, and improving. This is the essence of continuous feedback: an unending loop that connects employees, customers, and leadership to drive meaningful innovation.

Feedback is not just a tool; it's a philosophy. Businesses that embed feedback into their DNA don't merely survive - they thrive, transforming themselves into dynamic organisms that evolve with the world around them. To build and sustain such a culture, entrepreneurs must first grasp the multi-faceted power of feedback and the strategies for leveraging it effectively.

### The Anatomy of a Feedback Loop

At its simplest, a feedback loop consists of four steps: collecting insights, analyzing them, implementing changes, and measuring outcomes. This cycle may appear straightforward, but its success hinges on several factors, including trust, transparency, and a willingness to embrace vulnerability.

**1. Listening as a Skill**
Listening is an art, and it forms the cornerstone of any effective feedback loop. Entrepreneurs must cultivate the patience and humility to truly hear what stakeholders are saying - whether it's an employee's concern about workload or a customer's frustration with a product feature.

However, listening isn't passive. It involves probing deeper, asking clarifying questions, and reading between the lines to uncover underlying issues. A simple complaint about a delayed delivery, for instance, might reveal broader problems in supply chain management or communication systems.

**2. Analyzing with Objectivity**

Once feedback is collected, the next step is to sift through the data objectively. Not all feedback is actionable or relevant, and sifting the signal from the noise is a critical skill. Entrepreneurs must learn to separate constructive criticism from emotional venting and identify recurring patterns that point to systemic issues.

Data analytics tools can play a crucial role in this process. Platforms like Qualtrics or Salesforce enable businesses to organize and visualize feedback, making it easier to spot trends and prioritize initiatives.

**3. Acting with Precision**

Acting on feedback requires more than just good intentions; it demands focus and precision. Changes should be implemented in a way that aligns with the organization's vision and goals. For example, if customers consistently request a feature that deviates from your product's core purpose, it might be worth considering whether fulfilling that request would dilute your brand.

This step also requires transparency. When changes are made based on feedback, it's important to communicate the "why" behind those decisions. This builds trust and encourages further input.

**4. Measuring Impact and Iterating**

The feedback loop doesn't end once changes are implemented. Businesses must track the outcomes of their actions to determine whether they've addressed the original issues. If not, the loop begins anew, with lessons learned guiding the next iteration.

**Employee Feedback: The Silent Innovators**

While customer feedback often steals the spotlight, employee feedback is equally - if not more - critical. Employees are the frontline operators who interact with systems, customers, and processes daily. Their insights can uncover inefficiencies, inspire creative solutions, and illuminate cultural blind spots.

### The Role of Leadership in Employee Feedback

Leadership sets the tone for how feedback is handled within an organization. A leader who welcomes criticism with grace and curiosity creates a ripple effect, encouraging others to share openly. Conversely, leaders who dismiss or punish feedback risk creating a culture of silence, where problems fester until they become crises.

Consider Microsoft under Satya Nadella's leadership. When Nadella became CEO in 2014, he prioritized fostering a growth mindset across the company. He encouraged employees to share ideas, even if they were unconventional or unpolished. This cultural shift played a significant role in Microsoft's resurgence, driving innovations in cloud computing, artificial intelligence, and gaming.

### Practical Methods for Gathering Employee Feedback

**Pulse Surveys**: Short, frequent surveys that gauge employee sentiment on specific issues.

**One-on-One Check-Ins**: Regular meetings between managers and employees to discuss progress, challenges, and ideas.

**Suggestion Platforms**: Tools like Slack channels or dedicated apps where employees can submit and vote on ideas.

**Exit Interviews**: Conversations with departing employees can reveal systemic issues that might not surface otherwise.

But collecting feedback is only half the battle. Employees need to see tangible results from their input, or they'll stop participating. This is why closing the feedback loop - by acknowledging contributions and explaining how they're being addressed - is crucial.

### Customer Feedback: The North Star

Customers are the ultimate arbiters of a business's success. Their satisfaction - or lack thereof - can make or break a brand. Yet, collecting customer feedback is not enough; it must be analyzed and acted upon with a sense of urgency and purpose.

**Building Channels for Customer Feedback**
Companies that excel in leveraging customer feedback do so by meeting customers where they are. Traditional methods like surveys and focus groups are still valuable, but digital tools have expanded the possibilities.

**Social Media Monitoring**: Platforms like Twitter and Instagram provide unfiltered insights into customer opinions.

**Product Reviews**: Sites like Amazon and Yelp offer a wealth of data on customer preferences and pain points.

**In-App Feedback**: Apps and digital platforms can incorporate real-time feedback tools, such as star ratings or comment boxes.

**Case Study: Apple's Genius Bar**
Apple's Genius Bar is a masterclass in customer feedback integration. Customers visiting the store for repairs or advice are encouraged to share their experiences, which are then logged and analyzed. These insights inform everything from product design to store layout, ensuring that Apple remains one of the most customer-centric brands in the world.

**Feedback as a Springboard for Innovation**

Feedback doesn't just solve problems; it sparks creativity. Many of history's greatest innovations stemmed from addressing complaints or fulfilling unmet needs.

**From Complaint to Opportunity**
In the 1970s, customers complained that Post-it Notes didn't stick well enough to replace traditional adhesives. Instead of shelving the product, 3M turned this feedback into a unique selling point, marketing Post-its as repositionable notes. Today, they're a global staple in offices and homes.

**Feedback in Iterative Design**
The tech industry, in particular, thrives on iterative design fuelled by feedback. Agile development methodologies rely on constant input from users to refine products. This cycle of build-test-learn has produced world-changing technologies, from smartphones to cloud computing platforms.

## Creating a Feedback-Driven Culture

To make feedback a cornerstone of your business, it must permeate every level of your organization. This means cultivating a mindset where feedback is seen not as criticism but as an opportunity for growth.

### Principles of a Feedback-Driven Culture

**Openness**: Encourage candid discussions without fear of retribution.

**Actionability**: Focus on feedback that can lead to meaningful change.

**Accountability**: Assign clear ownership for implementing changes.

**Celebration**: Recognize and reward those who contribute valuable insights.

## Conclusion: The Future is Feedback

In the modern business landscape, feedback is not just a tool - it's a lifeline. Companies that prioritize listening and learning from their stakeholders will find themselves more agile, innovative, and resilient. As you continue your entrepreneurial journey, remember that feedback is not a sign of weakness; it's a testament to your commitment to excellence.

In the next chapter, we'll explore the art of storytelling in business - how crafting a compelling narrative can elevate your brand, inspire loyalty, and leave an indelible mark on your audience.

CHAPTER SEVENTEEN

# Funding Your Venture

Funding is the lifeblood of any venture, yet it is far more complex than merely securing a check. It is a journey that intertwines strategy, persistence, and adaptability, with each stage presenting unique challenges and opportunities. To truly master this aspect of entrepreneurship, one must delve deeply into the nuances of funding methods, the psychology of investors, and the evolving dynamics of capital markets.

Let us now explore further dimensions of funding that are critical for entrepreneurs to understand and implement effectively.

**Stages of Funding: The Entrepreneurial Milestones**

The funding journey of a business often unfolds in stages, each corresponding to a distinct phase of growth. These stages, while fluid, generally follow a trajectory from initial bootstrapping to larger institutional investments. Understanding these stages equips entrepreneurs with the knowledge to align their funding needs with their business goals.

**Bootstrapping: The Foundation of Resilience**

Bootstrapping, or self-funding, is the first and most personal form of funding. It demands that you dip into your savings, liquidate assets, or reinvest profits to sustain and grow your business. While this approach may seem daunting, it comes with unparalleled benefits - complete control over your venture, freedom from investor pressure, and a lean, cost-efficient operation.

Countless success stories are built on the foundation of bootstrapping. Dell Technologies, for instance, began in Michael Dell's college dorm room, funded by his personal savings. Bootstrapping not only instills financial discipline but also demonstrates to potential investors that you are willing to take significant risks for your vision - a compelling trait that can attract funding down the road.

**Seed Funding: Planting the Roots**

As your idea transitions into a tangible product or service, seed funding becomes the next logical step. This stage involves raising smaller amounts of capital, often from family, friends, or angel investors. These early supporters are not just financiers; they are believers in your potential and the first validators of your vision.

When seeking seed funding, focus on articulating your "why" - why your idea matters, why it will succeed, and why now is the time to act. Emphasize the potential impact of their investment, not just in monetary terms but also in terms of creating value for society.

**Series Funding: Scaling Up**

As your business gains traction, you may need to raise larger rounds of funding - Series A, B, C, and beyond. Each round serves a specific purpose: Series A might focus on market expansion, Series B on optimizing operations, and Series C on diversifying offerings or entering new markets. At this stage, professional investors such as venture capitalists and private equity firms become involved, bringing not only capital but also industry expertise and networks.

**Debt Financing: An Alternative Path**

Equity financing often garners the spotlight, but debt financing is an equally viable path, particularly for entrepreneurs who wish to retain ownership. Bank loans, credit lines, and government grants are common forms of debt financing. Unlike equity, debt must be repaid, making it a less attractive option for risk-averse entrepreneurs. However, for those with a solid business model and predictable cash flow, debt financing can be a strategic choice.

**Investor Perspectives: What They Look For**

To secure funding, it is essential to step into the shoes of potential investors. Whether they are angel investors, venture capitalists, or corporate backers, understanding their mindset can help you tailor your approach.

**Risk vs. Reward**

Investors are, at their core, risk-takers, but calculated ones. They evaluate potential returns against the inherent risks of your venture. Demonstrating a clear path to profitability, backed by data and a sound strategy, can tip the scales in your favour.

**The "X Factor"**

Beyond the metrics, investors often look for intangible qualities - the passion, resilience, and vision of the entrepreneur. Are you adaptable in the face of challenges? Do you have the charisma to inspire a team and attract customers? These qualities can be as influential as your financial projections.

**Traction and Metrics**

Traction - evidence of market demand for your product - is a critical factor in securing funding. It could be in the form of sales, partnerships, or even pre-orders. Metrics such as customer acquisition cost (CAC), lifetime value (LTV), and churn rate provide concrete evidence of your business's health and potential.

**Funding Challenges: Navigating the Obstacles**

The funding journey is rarely linear, and each stage comes with its own set of challenges. Being prepared for these obstacles can help you navigate them effectively.

**Rejection: A Rite of Passage**

Rejection is an inevitable part of the process. Even iconic entrepreneurs like Steve Jobs and Elon Musk faced countless rejections before securing their first big breaks. The key is to treat each rejection as a learning opportunity. Analyze the feedback, refine your pitch, and approach the next investor with renewed confidence.

**Dilution Dilemmas**

As you raise more rounds of funding, equity dilution becomes a concern. Balancing the need for capital with the desire to retain control requires careful planning. Seeking legal and financial advice during this stage can help you structure deals that align with your long-term goals.

**Economic Fluctuations**

Economic downturns and market instability can significantly impact funding availability. During such times, alternative funding sources, such as grants or strategic partnerships, can serve as lifelines. Maintaining financial prudence and building a cash reserve during prosperous times can also help you weather economic storms.

**Leveraging Feedback for Funding Success**

In the quest for funding, feedback becomes an invaluable tool. Whether it's from investors, customers, or mentors, constructive criticism can refine your pitch and strengthen your business model.

For instance, consider the journey of Warby Parker, the eyewear brand that revolutionized its industry. Early investor feedback prompted the founders to refine their value proposition, leading to the adoption of their now-famous "home try-on" program. This innovation not only won over customers but also made their business model more appealing to investors.

**Final Thoughts: A Journey of Persistence and Vision**

Funding is not just about raising money; it's about building relationships, validating your vision, and creating opportunities for growth. The process will test your resilience, challenge your assumptions, and refine your business acumen.

As you reflect on your funding journey, remember that each milestone is a testament to your determination and creativity. Every dollar you raise is an endorsement of your idea and a step closer to making your entrepreneurial dreams a reality.

In the next chapter, we'll shift our focus to the art of scaling your venture - transforming your startup into a sustainable, impactful enterprise that leaves a lasting legacy. The foundation you've built through thoughtful funding strategies will serve as the springboard for this next stage of growth.

# CHAPTER EIGHTEEN

# Scaling Without Losing Quality

Scaling a business is a critical milestone in an entrepreneur's journey. It signifies growth, expanding horizons, and the realization of ambitious goals. However, it is also a stage fraught with risks, as maintaining the quality of your products, services, and culture while growing is no small feat. For Indian entrepreneurs, scaling can be even more challenging due to diverse customer preferences, regional complexities, and varying market conditions across the nation.

This chapter dives into the nuances of scaling a business, drawing lessons from both global and Indian companies. We'll explore how to recognize the right time to scale, strategies for maintaining quality during growth, and how businesses in India have scaled successfully without losing their essence.

**Recognizing the Right Time to Scale**

The decision to scale must be rooted in careful analysis and readiness. Expanding too soon can dilute your brand, while waiting too long may lead to missed opportunities. Indian entrepreneurs often find themselves navigating unique challenges such as navigating bureaucracy, diverse consumer behaviors, and infrastructural limitations.

**1. Consistent Demand and Market Validation**
Before scaling, businesses must establish a steady and growing demand for their offerings. For instance, **Zomato**, the Indian food delivery and restaurant discovery platform, expanded its reach only after validating its business model in metropolitan cities. By understanding urban consumers' reliance on technology for convenience, Zomato ensured it had the demand to sustain its growth.

**2. Operational Efficiency**
Scaling multiplies both successes and inefficiencies. An operational bottleneck that is manageable for a small business can turn disastrous during rapid expansion. Companies like **Amul**, one of India's most iconic dairy brands, built a robust supply chain model before scaling. Amul's cooperative structure allowed it to efficiently source milk from millions of farmers, ensuring quality and consistency across its products while growing into a global brand.

**3. Financial and Resource Preparedness**
Expanding a business requires significant financial investment, whether for hiring, increasing production, or marketing. Indian startups like **OYO Rooms** raised substantial funding rounds to support their scaling efforts. Founder Ritesh Agarwal demonstrated how meticulous financial planning and securing the right investors are crucial for sustainable growth.

## Strategies for Maintaining Quality During Growth

For Indian businesses, quality and trust are often non-negotiable. Scaling without compromising on these pillars requires a fine balance of innovation, operational excellence, and customer focus.

### Investing in People and Processes
A skilled and motivated workforce is essential for delivering consistent quality. Companies like **Tata Consultancy Services (TCS)** prioritize employee training and development, ensuring their workforce is equipped to handle the challenges of scaling. By fostering a culture of continuous learning and empowerment, TCS maintained its reputation as a reliable IT solutions provider while expanding globally.

Standardizing processes also plays a crucial role. For example, **Reliance Retail** achieved rapid expansion by replicating a standardized operational model across various cities while catering to local tastes and preferences.

### Leveraging Technology for Growth
Technology can streamline operations and improve customer experiences during scaling. E-commerce giant **Flipkart** relied heavily on technology to handle logistics, inventory management, and customer support. By

investing in AI-driven solutions, Flipkart ensured scalability without compromising on delivery timelines or product availability.

**Adapting to Regional Preferences**

One of the biggest challenges Indian businesses faces while scaling is catering to diverse regional markets. **Big Bazaar**, the hypermarket chain, tailored its inventory to suit local tastes in different states, from carrying traditional spices in the South to featuring local snacks in Gujarat. This localization strategy allowed it to maintain relevance and customer loyalty across India.

**Preserving Company Culture During Expansion**

For entrepreneurs, scaling is not just about increasing revenue but also about growing their vision and values. Indian businesses often place significant emphasis on maintaining their ethos during growth.

**Building a Strong Organizational Ethos**

The **Infosys** story is a testament to the importance of culture in scaling. From its humble beginnings to becoming a global IT leader, Infosys stayed committed to its principles of integrity, transparency, and innovation. Regular communication of these values and consistent leadership have ensured that Infosys's culture remains intact even as its workforce has grown exponentially.

**Hiring for Cultural Fit**

The people you bring on board during scaling will define the future of your company. **Haldiram's**, one of India's largest snack brands, retained its authentic flavor and traditional recipes by hiring employees who understood its legacy. Simultaneously, it brought in professionals with modern expertise to scale its manufacturing and distribution.

**Lessons from Indian Businesses That Scaled Successfully**

**1. Dabur: Scaling with Tradition**

Dabur, an Ayurvedic FMCG giant, successfully scaled by staying true to its roots in natural and herbal products. Even as it diversified into health, personal care, and food products, Dabur ensured that its offerings were aligned with its core philosophy of Ayurveda. Its focus on innovation, such as introducing honey in easy-to-use squeeze packs, allowed it to cater to modern consumers without diluting its traditional essence.

**2. BYJU'S: EdTech Scaling with Purpose**
BYJU'S began as a small coaching class and scaled into the world's largest EdTech company by leveraging technology and creating a personalized learning experience for students. The company focused on maintaining the quality of its content even as it expanded globally, hiring subject matter experts and investing in immersive learning technologies.

**3. Jaipur Rugs: Combining Artisanship with Scale**
Jaipur Rugs, a social enterprise, scaled its operations while preserving the traditional craftsmanship of rural artisans. By creating a transparent supply chain and investing in community development, the company maintained its high standards of quality and ensured that the artisans benefited from its growth.

### Navigating Challenges Unique to Indian Markets

Scaling in India often comes with its unique hurdles, from infrastructural limitations to regulatory complexities. Successful businesses overcome these challenges by being resourceful and resilient.

**Regulatory Navigation**
The Indian regulatory environment can be daunting for growing businesses. Companies like **Paytm**, the digital payments platform, successfully navigated these challenges by building strong relationships with policymakers and staying ahead of compliance requirements.

**Overcoming Infrastructure Gaps**
For businesses operating in tier-2 and tier-3 cities, infrastructural challenges can hinder scaling efforts. **Lenskart**, the eyewear retailer, tackled this by developing a hybrid online and offline model, using technology to reach remote customers while ensuring a physical presence in key markets.

### Scaling as a Journey, Not a Destination

Scaling is not just about expanding operations; it is about sustaining excellence while growing. Indian entrepreneurs must navigate a diverse landscape, balancing innovation with tradition, and efficiency with personalization. By learning from successful examples and focusing on quality, culture, and customer satisfaction, you can ensure that your business scales sustainably and thrives in the long term.

As we transition to the next chapter, we will explore how to leverage innovation as a driver of sustainable growth, ensuring your business remains relevant and competitive in an ever-evolving market.

CHAPTER NINETEEN

# Measuring Success and KPIs

As an entrepreneur, I've always believed that success isn't just about achieving milestones - it's about sustaining growth, adapting to challenges, and constantly improving. In a world driven by data, measuring success requires more than intuition or passion. It demands a clear understanding of Key Performance Indicators (KPIs) and a commitment to learning from both triumphs and failures.

This chapter delves into how tracking the right metrics can fuel growth, prevent stagnation, and create a framework for innovation. Drawing from my personal journey and experiences, along with examples of other businesses, I'll share insights on how data-driven strategies have been instrumental in shaping my ventures.

**The Importance of Measuring Success**

Success is multifaceted. For me, it's not just about financial achievements but also about creating meaningful impact. Early in my entrepreneurial journey, I realized that without measurable goals, progress could easily plateau. The transition from dreaming about success to systematically achieving it required me to embrace data and metrics as allies.

When I founded **DevelopUs.tech**, a web development company, I knew that understanding client satisfaction, project efficiency, and team performance would be critical. My team and I developed systems to track delivery timelines, customer feedback, and project outcomes. These metrics didn't just tell us how we were performing; they showed us where we could do better.

### Identifying the Right KPIs for Your Business

Every business has unique goals, and the metrics you track should reflect those objectives. For instance, in web development, customer satisfaction and project delivery time are crucial. In contrast, my other ventures, such as **RKL Worlds** under the Samaroh Group, required metrics like product quality and market penetration.

Here's how I approached identifying the right KPIs:

> **Aligning with Core Objectives**
> I asked myself: What does success look like for this venture? For **DevelopUs.tech**, it was about delivering innovative solutions efficiently. This led to KPIs like customer retention rates and average project turnaround time.
>
> **Tracking Financial Health**
> Financial metrics like profit margins, cash flow, and ROI are universal indicators of business health. During the early days, I paid close attention to these metrics to ensure sustainability while reinvesting profits to scale operations.
>
> **Employee Engagement and Productivity**
> In my experience, a motivated team is the backbone of success. At **RKL Worlds**, my focus extended to tracking employee satisfaction, training outcomes, and retention rates. A team that feels valued delivers exceptional results.

### Success Stories of Startups Using Data-Driven Strategies

India is brimming with examples of businesses that have leveraged KPIs to scale and thrive. Take **Flipkart**, for instance. The company revolutionized e-commerce by meticulously tracking customer acquisition costs, delivery timelines, and user satisfaction scores. Their data-driven approach allowed them to fine-tune operations and outpace competitors.

Similarly, **Zomato**, which began as a restaurant review platform, used metrics like user engagement and app downloads to pivot into food delivery. This transition wouldn't have been possible without a deep understanding of their data.

On a personal level, my ventures have also benefited from data-driven insights. For instance, when expanding **DevelopUs.tech**, we noticed that repeat clients accounted for a significant portion of our revenue. This insight led us to focus on nurturing long-term relationships, offering loyalty programs, and prioritizing post-project support.

## Lessons from My Own Journey

When I look back on my journey from a small fishing village in Rajegaon to leading multiple ventures, I realize that every step was guided by metrics - whether I recognized them at the time or not.

During my diploma in computer engineering, I participated in Project Mania competitions every semester. Winning consistently required evaluating what worked and refining my approach. This habit of self-assessment translated seamlessly into my professional life.

When I launched **Samaroh Group of Business and Industries**, which now encompasses multiple companies, I knew the stakes were higher. Success here wasn't just about individual achievements but about building a legacy. Metrics like market share, customer reach, and team scalability became vital in guiding our expansion.

One memorable instance was when I introduced a new service line at **DevelopUs.tech**. The initial response was underwhelming. Instead of scrapping the idea, I analyzed customer feedback, improved the offering, and relaunched it with a targeted marketing strategy. The result? A 30% increase in project inquiries within the first month.

## Balancing Data with Intuition

While KPIs are invaluable, I've learned not to let them overshadow intuition. Numbers tell a story, but they don't capture everything. For example, when expanding into new markets, I've relied on a mix of data and gut feeling. Understanding customer needs, cultural nuances, and emerging trends often requires more than analytics.

For instance, while data showed a high demand for tech services in metro cities, I chose to explore tier-2 cities as well. This decision was rooted in my belief that emerging markets held untapped potential - a belief that proved right when smaller cities contributed significantly to our revenue growth.

### How to Avoid Stagnation

One of the biggest threats to any business is complacency. Over time, it's easy to rely on past successes and lose the drive to innovate. Here are strategies that have helped me avoid stagnation:

**Embrace Continuous Feedback**
At all my companies, from **DevelopUs.tech** to **RKL Worlds**, we have systems for gathering feedback from employees and clients. Constructive criticism is a goldmine for innovation.

**Revisit and Revise KPIs**
What worked yesterday might not work tomorrow. I regularly evaluate whether our metrics align with our evolving goals. For example, as we expanded into international markets, we added KPIs like geographic penetration and global client retention rates.

**Invest in Learning and Development**
I've always believed that growth begins with people. By upskilling teams and staying updated on industry trends, we ensure that stagnation doesn't creep into our operations.

### Looking Ahead

Measuring success isn't a one-time task; it's an ongoing process. As I continue to lead my ventures, I remain committed to balancing ambition with accountability. By tracking progress, learning from data, and staying adaptable, I aim to ensure that success isn't just a fleeting moment but a sustainable journey.

In the next chapter, we'll explore how to balance ambition with mindfulness, ensuring that the entrepreneurial journey remains fulfilling, purposeful, and aligned with personal well-being.

CHAPTER TWENTY

# The Lifelong Journey of an Entrepreneur

Entrepreneurship is a journey, not a destination. It's a path filled with unexpected twists, turns, and challenges that test your will, shape your character, and ultimately, determine the legacy you leave behind. As I sit here reflecting on my journey - starting from a small village in Rajegaon to founding and leading multiple companies - I realize that entrepreneurship has taught me much more than just business skills. It has shaped my entire outlook on life, my values, and the way I see success. It has instilled in me the belief that success is not an end goal but a continuous process - a journey of relentless pursuit, learning, and growth.

Through every challenge, I've learned that staying inspired and committed to your vision is crucial. Even when the road seems long and daunting, it is essential to hold on to that one thing that keeps you going: your purpose. The same principle has been true for countless entrepreneurs who have come before me, who faced insurmountable odds yet left behind legacies that have shaped industries and inspired generations.

As I reflect on this lifelong journey, I want to share not only my experiences but also the stories of some of the world's most iconic entrepreneurs whose resilience and ability to adapt have made them giants in their fields. These entrepreneurs didn't just achieve financial success - they changed the world in ways that continue to impact us today. Their stories serve as a powerful reminder that the path of entrepreneurship is not just about the destination, but about the perseverance to keep moving forward.

**Staying Inspired Through Evolving Challenges**

Entrepreneurship is an unpredictable path - filled with challenges that are often bigger than you can imagine. The way you respond to these challenges is what defines you as an entrepreneur. There will be times when things seem to be falling apart, when it feels like you've hit a wall, but the entrepreneurs who make it through these moments are the ones who find inspiration even in the darkest of times. For me, the moments of greatest adversity often became the moments of greatest growth.

When I first started **DevelopUs.tech**, there were days when everything seemed uncertain. Being from a small town in India, with limited resources and a steep learning curve, it was easy to question my decision to enter the world of technology and entrepreneurship. But there was something deeper driving me - something beyond money or recognition. It was the vision of creating a platform that could bring digital transformation to businesses around the world. That vision kept me grounded and focused, no matter how tough things got.

A similar story of resilience comes from **Elon Musk**, the founder of **Tesla**, **SpaceX**, and **Neuralink**. Musk faced tremendous challenges, especially when Tesla was on the brink of bankruptcy in 2008. There was a time when many believed that his dreams of revolutionizing the electric vehicle industry were far-fetched. Yet Musk refused to give up. His passion for sustainable energy and space exploration kept him going through those dark days. He once famously said, "When something is important enough, you do it even if the odds are not in your favour." Musk's story teaches us that it is not the absence of challenges but the determination to overcome them that makes an entrepreneur successful.

Similarly, **Steve Jobs**, co-founder of **Apple**, was fired from the very company he built - a huge blow to any entrepreneur's ego. Yet, his eventual return to Apple led to the transformation of not only the company but the tech industry as a whole. Jobs understood the importance of staying inspired even when faced with seemingly insurmountable challenges. He once said, "You can't connect the dots looking forward; you can only connect them looking backward." It was his ability to learn from failure and continue innovating that made him one of the most iconic entrepreneurs of our time.

## Celebrating Milestones While Preparing for the Future

The entrepreneurial journey is filled with milestones - each one marking a significant achievement. But one of the greatest lessons I've learned is that success should never be seen as the end. Each milestone is simply a step forward in a larger journey. It is important to celebrate these achievements, but it is equally essential to continue focusing on what comes next. The key to longevity in entrepreneurship is the ability to continuously adapt and evolve.

In my own story, after founding **DevelopUs.tech**, our first successful project was a moment of immense pride. It validated everything I had worked for and proved that we could deliver high-quality digital solutions. But that moment of success wasn't the finish line - it was just the beginning. Each project we completed taught me something new and pushed me to improve, to think bigger, and to dream beyond what was immediately achievable. Success, I realized, wasn't just about what we had accomplished; it was about how much further we could go.

**Ratan Tata**, the former chairman of **Tata Group**, shares this philosophy of constant growth. Under his leadership, Tata Group transformed into one of the largest conglomerates in India, but Tata was never one to rest on his laurels. He led acquisitions of companies like **Jaguar Land Rover** and **Corus Steel**, ensuring the company adapted to a globalized market. Even in his retirement, Tata continues to contribute to the growth of India, focusing on philanthropy and innovation. His ability to pivot and think globally serves as a great lesson in entrepreneurship: never stop growing, even when success seems within reach.

Another example is **Indra Nooyi**, the former CEO of **PepsiCo**, who took the company to new heights through her strategic vision and focus on healthier products. Nooyi's leadership shows that it's not enough to be content with where you are; true success lies in preparing for the future while celebrating the present. Her legacy is a testament to the power of visionary leadership and the importance of staying agile and forward-thinking.

## Profiles of Enduring Entrepreneurs and Their Legacies

The most successful entrepreneurs are those who leave behind more than just financial success - they leave legacies that continue to impact future generations. These entrepreneurs change the way we think, live, and interact with the world.

**Dhirubhai Ambani**, the founder of **Reliance Industries**, built an empire that revolutionized the Indian petrochemical industry and later, telecommunications. He was a self-made entrepreneur who started with nothing, working his way up from a small village in Gujarat to building one of India's largest conglomerates. Ambani's legacy is built on his unwavering belief that anyone, regardless of their background, can achieve success with determination and vision. His story is a reminder that greatness can emerge from the most unlikely of places, and that entrepreneurship is about more than wealth - it's about creating lasting change.

In the world of technology, **Bill Gates**, the co-founder of **Microsoft**, is another entrepreneur whose legacy continues to inspire. Gates' success isn't just about the personal wealth he amassed but also about the way he revolutionized personal computing. Beyond Microsoft, his philanthropic efforts through the **Bill & Melinda Gates Foundation** have impacted millions of lives around the world, demonstrating that true success is not just measured in profits but in the positive change you bring to the world.

Similarly, **Oprah Winfrey**, who turned a career in television into a global media empire, exemplifies the power of perseverance and personal growth. Winfrey's story is a powerful reminder that entrepreneurship can be about more than business; it's about creating something that connects deeply with people and adds value to their lives.

Even today, **Jeff Bezos** of **Amazon**, **Mark Zuckerberg** of **Facebook**, and **Brian Chesky** of **Airbnb** continue to reshape industries and challenge conventional norms. Each of them built companies that disrupted traditional business models and transformed entire sectors, but they all share one common trait: the relentless pursuit of innovation. They understood that entrepreneurship is not just about competing; it's about thinking differently and creating something that has a profound impact on society.

**The Lifelong Commitment to Learning and Adaptability**

One of the greatest lessons I've learned as an entrepreneur is that the journey is never static. The world, the economy, and technology are always evolving, and if you want to remain relevant, you must continue learning and adapting. Entrepreneurship is about change - change in how you do business, change in how you think, and change in how you approach challenges. Those who thrive are those who see change not as an obstacle, but as an opportunity.

For me, continuous learning has been a cornerstone of my entrepreneurial journey. Whether it's mastering new technologies like **React JS**, **Node JS**, and **MongoDB**, or understanding the latest trends in the business world, I've always sought to expand my knowledge and adapt to new challenges. The tech world, in particular, moves at a rapid pace, and staying ahead requires constant learning and upskilling.

This commitment to learning is something that all successful entrepreneurs have in common. **Elon Musk**, for example, isn't just a visionary; he's also an avid learner who has taught himself everything from rocket science to artificial intelligence. His ability to absorb knowledge from various disciplines has been crucial in his ventures, enabling him to push the boundaries of what's possible.

## Conclusion: The End of One Journey, The Beginning of Another

As I look back on my entrepreneurial journey, I realize that it has been an ongoing process of growth, learning, and transformation. The milestones I have achieved, while meaningful, are just the beginning of what I hope will be a lifelong journey of innovation, leadership, and impact. The entrepreneurial journey is about more than just success - it's about having the courage to pursue your dreams, the resilience to overcome setbacks, and the vision to see what others cannot.

In closing, I encourage you to embrace the lifelong journey of entrepreneurship with all its challenges, triumphs, and opportunities. Don't let fear of failure stop you from pursuing your dreams. Celebrate each milestone, but always keep looking ahead. Learn from the giants who came before you, but carve out your own path. Your journey is unique, and the world needs your vision. The road may be long, but it is filled with endless possibilities. May you find the inspiration to keep moving forward, no matter where your journey takes you.

Remember, the real success of an entrepreneur isn't in what they achieve but in how they impact the world and inspire future generations to chase their dreams. Your legacy begins today.

FINAL THOUGHTS

# FROM THE HEART OF AN ENTREPRENEUR

As this book reaches its closing pages, I find myself reflecting on the journey that led to its creation - a journey filled with challenges, learning, and growth. Writing ***The Entrepreneur's Blueprint*** has been an incredibly fulfilling experience, offering me the chance to share not only my strategies for success but also the values and lessons that shaped my entrepreneurial path.

This book is not the end of our journey - it's a beginning. Whether you're an aspiring entrepreneur, a seasoned professional, or someone searching for inspiration, the insights here are meant to guide you, motivate you, and remind you that success is a continuous journey. It's about dreaming big, staying resilient, and embracing each setback as a stepping stone.

To everyone who picks up this book: thank you. Your trust and curiosity inspire me to keep pushing boundaries and reaching for new heights.

If this book has sparked ideas or questions, I would love to stay connected. Follow me on my social media platforms for more insights, updates, and inspiration:

**INSTAGRAM :** *@CEOROHAN*
**LINKEDIN :** *ROHAN KUMAR BHOI*
**TWITTER/X :** *CEOROHAN1*
**FACEBOOK :** *CEOROHAN*

Let's continue building dreams, one step at a time.

**To the dreamers and doers,**
*Your journey is yours to create. Go forward boldly.*

Warm regards,
**Rohan Kumar Bhoi**
Founder & Chairman,
Samaroh Group of Business and Industries

www.ingramcontent.com/pod-product-compliance
Lightning Source LLC
LaVergne TN
LVHW091057150826
845673LV00002B/616

* 9 7 9 8 8 9 6 7 3 2 7 5 4 *